TWENTIETH CENTURY VIEWS

The aim of this series is to present the best in contemporary critical opinion on major authors, providing a twentieth century perspective on their changing status in an era of profound revaluation.

Maynard Mack, *Series Editor*
Yale University

WOMEN WRITERS
OF THE
SHORT STORY

WOMEN WRITERS OF THE SHORT STORY

A COLLECTION OF CRITICAL ESSAYS

Edited by
Heather McClave

Prentice-Hall, Inc. *Englewood Cliffs, N.J.*

A SPECTRUM BOOK

Library of Congress Cataloging in Publication Data

MAIN ENTRY UNDER TITLE:

Women writers of the short story.

    (Twentieth century views) (A Spectrum Book)
    Bibliography: p.
    CONTENTS: McClave, H. Introduction.—Berthoff, W.
The art of Jewett's Pointed firs.—Lewis, R. W. B.
Introduction to The collected short stories of
Edith Wharton. [etc.]
    1. Short stories, American—Women authors—History
and criticism—Addresses, essays, lectures.
I. McClave, Heather.
PS374.S5W6   823'.01   79-22917
ISBN 0-13-962415-5
ISBN 0-13-962407-4 pbk.

Editorial production/supervision by Heath Silberfeld
Woodcut: Vivian Berger, "The Displaced Person"
Manufacturing buyer: Barbara A. Frick

10   9   8   7   6   5   4   3   2   1

PRENTICE-HALL INTERNATIONAL, INC., *London*
PRENTICE-HALL OF AUSTRALIA PTY. LIMITED, *Sydney*
PRENTICE-HALL OF CANADA, LTD., *Toronto*
PRENTICE-HALL OF INDIA PRIVATE LIMITED, *New Delhi*
PRENTICE-HALL OF JAPAN, INC., *Tokyo*
PRENTICE-HALL OF SOUTHEAST ASIA PTE. LTD., *Singapore*
WHITEHALL BOOKS LIMITED, *Wellington, New Zealand*

For coming generations
of women writers
and their critics

Contents

Acknowledgements

Quotations from Katherine Anne Porter's "Flowering Judas," "The Cracked Looking-Glass," "Noon Wine," and "Old Mortality" are reprinted by permission of Harcourt Brace Jovanovich, Inc. (from *Flowering Judas and Other Stories* and *Pale Horse, Pale Rider*) and Jonathan Cape Ltd. (from *The Collected Stories of Katherine Anne Porter*). Copyright © 1965 by Katherine Anne Porter.

WOMEN WRITERS
OF THE
SHORT STORY

Introduction

by Heather McClave

I

When major writers emerge from what generally is considered a minor genre, we must reassess our critical judgments and return to the texts as inquiring readers. To date, short stories never have received the detailed academic attention devoted to poetry, plays, essays, and novels; but then in the history of literature they are comparatively new to the scene. Though short stories surely derive from the most ancient literary activities of telling anecdotes, folk tales, and fables, they appear as a distinctive written genre predominantly in the nineteenth century, where they take on varying attributes as "sketches," "tales," and "stories."

It would not be too startling to say that this latter-day short story is virtually an American form, adopted and developed fairly early by writers such as Irving, Hawthorne, Poe, and Melville and refined later by writers such as Howells, James, and Wharton, who draw on additional English, French, and Russian sources. Poe, an incisive and provocative practitioner-critic of short fiction, sets out a number of aims and means of what he calls "tales" when he reviews some of Hawthorne's work during the 1840s. The primary aim of the tale, he says, is "Truth," which can take in "a vast variety of modes of inflections of thought and expression" which would be unacceptable in the more rarefied poem where one must cultivate "Beauty." This human truth, which Poe also terms "earnestness or verisimilitude," can have "immense force" when it comes from a concentrated experience of *"totality,"* the experience of reading whole at one sitting a story that achieves a persuasive "single *effect.*"

Such key words as "Truth," "Beauty," "force," and *"totality"* should alert us to familiar Romantic values that underlie Poe's directives: the search for subjective intensity, for example; the sense of the mind's power to encompass the world it sees and to compress it into a Wordsworthian "spot of time"; the Platonic confidence that truth is absolute and inclusive, an ultimate *"totality"* through which the part (a "single *effect"*) can evoke and confirm the whole. Forty years later, these values lead plausibly enough to the subtle psychological and aesthetic treatments of "reality" that we find in Henry James, who resolves to give "a personal, a direct impression of life." And forty years after that, they inform the broken surfaces and mythic depths we meet in the modernists who have had the greatest influence on the literary style and perspective of our own time: Joyce, Pound, and Eliot. The short story, like the lyric poem, embodies the completed moment: immediate, self-contained, isolated from causal chains of events—much like the modern image of consciousness itself.

Within this large generic frame, and beyond it, we are concerned here with six outstanding short story writers from the nineteenth and twentieth centuries: Sarah Orne Jewett, Edith Wharton, Willa Cather, Katherine Anne Porter, Eudora Welty, and Flannery O'Connor. When we approach them as short story writers, or as Americans, or as regionalists of different sorts, we can avail ourselves of known contexts of criticism and history. When we try to distinguish their qualities as *women* writers, however—as women creating a literature of their own in the face of a male tradition that for so long has made women its foils, its mirrors, muses, and burdens—we enter a critical limbo where no clear standards exist. What vision of the world do these women contribute, and how does it compare with the vision we associate with American literature—a literature so deeply preoccupied with the struggles of men alone? How do these women seem to relate to the received tradition: do they identify with it, adapt it to their needs, reject it, or ignore it? Can we trace particular lines of continuity between women writers that suggest patterns of influence?

Questions such as these provide new and engaging issues, if not yet definitive answers. To ask them is to read with a larger sense of ourselves and to respond to a wider range of expression. We can begin by saying rather pointedly to the American secondary schools that tend to teach short stories and to the American colleges that tend to replace them with English novels that there is more to this genre than Crane, Faulkner, and Hemingway. Having read stories by the authors examined in this volume or by the many others remaining popularly at large—Kate Chopin, Mary Wilkins Freeman, Kay Boyle, Tess Slesinger, Tillie Olsen, Jean Stafford, Grace Paley, and Alice Walker come readily to mind—we find other voices, and with them, other options for our lives.

At this time it seems difficult to separate what may be a distinctive female sensibility from the culture as a whole. We may note with interest and perhaps some irony that what used to be the mission of hostile and curious critics who would dissect subject and style in order to posit female traits has now become a remedial imperative for feminists who seek an "authentic" female identity. Now as before, this effort seems more rhetorical than substantive, a shift in dialect and intonation, a narrowing of the field into fixed expectations. If women writers are to be viewed as exceptionally "sensitive" rather than as alarmingly "hysterical," there is still more left out than kept in.

Current studies which argue that women writers tend to be more unassuming in authorial voice or more antiheroic in attitude than their male counterparts fail to recognize the direct parallels between such aspects and the basic characteristics of modernism. Broadly, we could say that the proliferation of women writers from the mid-nineteenth century on coincides with the development of modernism as we know it. Features that we might anticipate in women writers, given their cultural restrictions, occur equally during this period in works by men: for example, the disappearance of a controlling authorial voice; the emphasis on subjective points of view, fractional and momentary; intense self-consciousness combined with the sense of being alienated from society and tradition; skepticism and anxiety about the nature and meaning of "progress"; images of passivity, impoverishment, and confinement. We find these things in Henry James, or in the dramatic monologues of Tennyson and Browning that culminate in *The Waste Land,* as well as in representative women writers.

A sense of universal loss and suspension, a sense of expanding hollowness both in the self and in civilization, tempers much of the literature of this period. As social cohesion seems to break down, journalistic attention to everyday detail and social criti-

cism give way to a more inward focus that depends on what
Eudora Welty (speaking of Katherine Anne Porter in "The Eye
of the Story") calls *"memory* imagery": imagery from a private
realm where experience crystallizes into static and primitive
objects, the bases of myth. Dickens gives way to Joyce in this
model, as George Eliot gives way to Woolf. As Welty aptly says
in her story, "The Wide Net," "when you go looking for what is
lost, everything is a sign." Early in the twentieth century, Freud's
genius is to suggest a method for the social process he observes as
once again people learn to search for meaning among their dreams.

It may be that within this context of certain themes and techniques, women writers emphasize particular values. Among the
writers featured here, all but O'Connor—who works to strip away
whatever intervenes between the individual soul and violent
Grace—link personal identity and survival to complicated ties to
a place, other people, a shared code of behavior, a history. For
them, typically, an escape to some lonely vigil in the wilderness
serves to *avoid* responsible endurance instead of teaching or
proving it. One comes to know oneself most deeply, and most
painfully, in relationship.

II

By the 1850s, women writers of the short story in America and
England are able to cultivate a vast and significantly female
readership by publishing in popular magazines which carry four
or five selections in any given issue. Established critics and
writers such as Hawthorne castigate these intrusive hordes of
"scribbling women" with a revulsion similar to what some con-
templative people today feel toward romantic fiction, television
serials, and canned Muzak. Few artists look forward to the erosion
of their appeal: the defense these early men make of their sexual
and territorial privilege must also be seen as a reaction against the
mass marketing of more casual, formulaic literature relying on
standard plots infused with sentimental and didactic clichés.

Indeed, the importance of many of these scribbling women has
little to do with art but much to do with history. Accustomed as
we are now to a more egalitarian climate, we forget too easily that
in the 1850s women can not yet go to college, or speak freely in

public, or choose a profession, or vote in general elections. To be published at all, they must devise an acceptable code. Yet they write in large numbers, using their own names, recording their own experiences. They show under pressure that women *can* write, not only as exceptional geniuses but also as commercially successful hacks. Thus they open the field for a new tradition.

As a genre, the short story requires a careful selection of material to convey meaning within strict limits on time and space. Each word must count. The attitude and approach must be clear. Instead of the epic overviews and slow accretion of details common to novels, short stories present the close and immediate scrutiny of a few subjects. They do not foster the illusion that we know everything: a scene, a brief encounter, a gesture can be enough—can be, as we say, *telling*. In theory, all we need to know —where knowing is a matter more of subjective inference than of objective evidence—already exists in the life we have and see.

Here again, sensibility takes precedence over experience in terms not only of form but also of content. Unlike the figure of Tiresias in *The Waste Land,* we need not have foresuffered all at length to understand a great deal about the world. As Jewett, Cather, and O'Connor all remark, if we have survived our childhood we have enough material to last us the rest of our lives.

Yet does anything last beyond that? Those such as Jewett, Wharton, and O'Connor, who would not grant total authority to the past or to private discretion tend to strengthen the role of archetypes and institutions that seem to have some universal bearing: the stoicism of human character and the bonds of family and community in Jewett; the regulations of society in Wharton; the mysterious certainty of divine justice in O'Connor. Others such as Cather, Porter, and Welty often allow more exposure to successive levels of underlying tension and uncertainty. As Cather says in her essay on Katherine Mansfield in *Not Under Forty,* "One realizes that human relationships are the tragic necessity of human life; that they can never be wholly satisfactory, that every ego is half the time greedily seeking them, and half the time pulling away from them."

Each of these writers offers a distinct approach to her craft. In her letters, Jewett stresses the importance of point of view and the depth of remembered experience that generates it. Wharton, in *The Writing of Fiction,* argues the need for a concrete situation in which essential character can be revealed, dismissing mere stream-of-consciousness as too insular and arbitrary a technique by itself. Whatever goes on in our minds, she advises us evenly, life has actual laws, "fairly coherent and selective lines," which we must take into account:

> ...only thus can the great fundamental affairs of bread-getting and home-and-tribe organizing be carried on. Drama, situation, is made out of the conflicts thus produced between social order and individual appetites, and the art of rendering life in fiction can never, in the last analysis, be anything, or need to be anything, but the disengaging of crucial moments from the welter of existence.[1]

Addressing the Balzacian realism that seems to catalogue disparate facts without incorporating them into a meaningful human whole, Cather in her essay "The Novel Démeublé" insists that art is something other than descriptive journalism, something more selective and compelling. Porter in her Paris journal of 1936 echoes Jewett in her emphasis on the personal aspects of writing which demand a "constant exercise of memory" to yield the raw material for fiction. In her essays "On Writing," "Writing and Analyzing a Story," and "Place in Fiction," Welty deals with several elements in turn: the ordering of the story; the allowance for mystery in human relationships; the crucial effect of place in defining a context of character; the primacy of feeling. O'Connor, in the occasional prose collected in *Mystery and Manners,* calls fiction "an incarnational art" which combines matter with spiritual mystery and which at its best embodies all dimensions of being.

As we consider these people grouped together not because of any explicit affinity but rather because they are especially fine examples of American women short story writers, we inevitably look for common themes. Their life patterns are unusual for American women, though less so for writers of their time. Only two of the six, Wharton and Porter, ever marry, and both are divorced. None, to my knowledge, have children.

It is not surprising that most of these women focus on struggles between individuals and their families or societies, reflecting per-

[1]Edith Wharton, *The Writing of Fiction* (New York: Octagon Books, Inc., 1966), pp. 13-14.

haps not only the ambivalence of the period toward authority but also the conflicting demands on women who would be artists. According to cultural stereotypes, women give while artists take; women *are* images, whereas artists make them. The curious absence of such struggles in Jewett seems more like displacement than achieved calm: her vision of isolated worlds controlled by older women, similar to what we find in feminist literature at the turn of the century, suggests a veneration of the female principle—women as earth mother, as witch, as sibyl, as obedient daughter, as observing consciousness—that excludes the processes of intercourse and childbirth.

Despite particular moments in Porter and Welty, all of these writers tend to minimize sexual identity and dramatically sexual problems, concentrating instead on such issues as the power and value of tradition; moral quandaries and tests of character; self-fulfillment and its limits in relation to the world; emotional bonds and deprivation. Plot, even in Wharton, the lady of situations, has little to do with surface action, so that little can be predicted. We can never describe the events of these stories and capture the feeling they convey. Instead, we become absorbed in the diverse currents these characters set up and submit to, currents which carry an undertow drag toward hidden and sometimes forbidden dimensions.

What seems especially striking when we look at a national literature filled with male protagonists who are resolutely on their own and whose heroic virtue depends in part on leaving women behind is that these writers, like their female predecessors, feature a range of women prominently in their stories: Jewett's Mrs. Todd in *The Country of the Pointed Firs;* /Wharton's upper-class wives and mistresses; Cather's "Old Mrs. Harris," or her grandes dames Myra Henshawe in *My Mortal Enemy* and "The Old Beauty"; Porter's fictional alter ego, Miranda; Welty's wonderful Old Phoenix in "A Worn Path," as well as her angry, crazy, retarded, fugitive counterparts in other stories; O'Connor's massive farm woman visionary, Mrs. Shortly in "The Displaced Person," her chronically anxious landowners, her hard, selfish mothers and vengeful children. Through these and other figures we see different sides of the human experience, often intensely confined, domestic, morally self-reflective. Women here, as elsewhere in literature, usually appear to be static, self-resolved for better or worse—working to conserve what they have, enduring painful or destructive change with measured grace or rage, committed to making do.

III

Critics have yet to examine short stories on a continuing basis. What studies we have, which still are few, come from a special interest in the subject and often take on a personal tone.

The essays collected in this volume are, to my mind, exemplary and definitive. Each has the freshness of a direct response to the work, and several add an engaging and intimate sense of the author. More than half are written by those who themselves have published fiction and poetry—Katherine Anne Porter, Lionel Trilling, Robert Penn Warren, Eudora Welty, Robert Fitzgerald, Thomas Merton, Joyce Carol Oates. All propose more an ongoing dialogue with their subjects and with other readers than a comprehensive theory.

Within this group, critical approaches vary along traditional lines: sociohistorical (Berthoff, Trilling); generally thematic (Lewis, Jones, Oates); thematic with textual analysis (Warren, Welty, Quinn); biographical and thematic (Porter, Fitzgerald); and philosophical (Merton). These remain the preferred modes of inquiry in the field. Persuasive studies of these authors from more current points of view—notably Marxist, psychological, structuralist, or feminist—have yet to appear.

The New Critical thinking that characterizes the thematic and textual analysis in many of the selections offered here has special relevance to literature by women. Until the twentieth century, "lady writers" are essentially relegated to a separate class where they are compared mainly with their own kind (enshrined as Jane Austen) and assessed in terms that duplicate and reinforce existing social codes of behavior. According to these rules, women should be delicate, wittily diverting, and modestly restrained in both speech and subject. Women praised for these achievements, however, are simultaneously demeaned for their slighter skills: "pretty" writing, by definition, can hardly be regarded as important work.

With its primary emphasis on text rather than context—on the integrity or "organic unity" of the individual work rather than its role in auxiliary systems of genres, social mores, or literary history—New Criticism brings a more impersonal set of standards to the task of interpreting literature. In effect, writing takes on a life of its own with distinctive form, pulse, and patterns of imagery. It becomes in quite a radical way a pure object: created, thus part of a particular time, place, and human consciousness, yet also self-contained, removed from the flux of the process world. During a period when peripheral things seem to be falling apart, art seems the center that holds.

The rise of New Criticism, deeply allied to modernist ideals of the impersonality of the artist and the intrinsic significance of myth and art, coincides with a new surge of feminist self-awareness and activity marked by the passage of women's suffrage in 1920. It may be that New Criticism, with its insular conception of art, serves more as a retrenchment than an advance in the face of social change. Yet at least in theory, women gain the option of being judged as artists first, and overall they seem to grow in confidence and stature in this professional role.

Not every woman, of course, embraces this future. Cather, like her predecessors, Wharton and Jewett, looks backward and chooses the past, when, as she says in *Not Under Forty*, "The world broke in two in 1922 or thereabouts."

The past two decades have registered a predictable shift in opinion toward contextual influences accompanied by nagging doubts about any permanence of meaning and value. Literature, by these lights, seems more arbitrary, episodic, and confessional. Once again, women, still seen as the *other* in this culture, are read as representative speakers for their sex.

Perhaps some good may come of this, if critics find definite grounds for a female tradition in literature, and if writers allow their imaginations to explore new territories. Already, we are encouraged to read what women have written with heightened interest and sympathy. For example, we may view Jewett's Country of the Pointed Firs not only as an actual world impoverished by its lack of vigorous men, as Professor Berthoff describes it, but also as a wishful vision of an alternate world, both primal and apocalyptic, where women appear close, powerful, and self-sufficient. Equally we could speculate that what Professor Trilling notes with such disdain in Cather—her need to attach "a mystical significance to the ritual of the ordered life, to the niceties of cookery, to the supernal virtues of *things* themselves—sherry, or lettuce"—may reflect a larger cultural problem for women who try to invest their own lives with personal meaning instead of merely accepting the attributions of conventional symbolism.

In art as in life, there are many more questions than answers. The essays and excerpts assembled in this volume provide a wide range of responses to the work, persons, and times of six major American writers. Like all good criticism, they help train our sensitivity to close and connotative reading without confounding it. They remain fine first statements on remarkable stories that have only begun to attract the serious audience they deserve.

The Art of Jewett's *Pointed Firs*

by Warner Berthoff

Somewhat of a curiosity in American letters, the considerable reputation of Sarah Orne Jewett's *The Country of the Pointed Firs* survives and holds its own in a less and less congenial era — as the best work of a scrupulous minor artist forgivably over-praised by personal admirers, a "little masterpiece" (Edward Garnett's verdict) but within the limits of the "local color" school. Willa Cather's generous estimate is the noted instance and may serve to remind us of the claims that have been made for the book. What she said has the ring of extravagance:

> If I were asked to name three American books which have the possibility of a long life, I would say at once, *The Scarlet Letter*, *Huckleberry Finn*, and *The Country of the Pointed Firs*. I can think of no others that confront time and change so serenely.

She wrote this in 1925 to introduce her own selection of Jewett's work, in devotion to an older writer who had befriended her at the start of her own career. In other circumstances would she have claimed as much? In the expanded version of her introduction published eleven years later in *Not Under Forty* these sentences are omitted.

But before discounting them we ought to consider what precisely they assert. Miss Cather was claiming for *Pointed Firs* a special quality — not of magnitude or power or importance but of durability, of freedom from vicissitudes of taste, therefore presumably of artistic wholeness. To make her point she invoked for

"The Art of Jewett's *Pointed Firs*" by Warner Berthoff. From *New England Quarterly*, XXXII (March 1959), 31-53. Reprinted by permission of *New England Quarterly*.

comparison two books which, like Jewett's, are distinctly "regional" but which possess, each in its own way, a formal coherence, a consistent intensity, that transcend their particular substance and setting. The achievement is one for which Willa Cather would have had a personal and professional respect, her novels being aimed (less successfully) at some such category of transcended regionalism. Grouping *Pointed Firs* with the masterpieces of Hawthorne and Mark Twain was her instinctive tribute to the American masters in her chosen province. It was by concentration on the local, the long familiar, the particular, that each had achieved the formal authority which is the precondition of significance as well as of permanence.

On the other hand, each had had to find his bearings as an artist and performer (no quick process) and to approach his material from a broader ground of experience, before the crowning achievement was possible. "One must know the world *so well* before one can know the parish," Sarah Jewett once wrote to Willa Cather (in context less sententiously, Cather tells us, than it may sound).[1] As such knowledge is measured Sarah Jewett, though she had lived as much in Boston as in Maine and had travelled abroad, scarcely knew the world well. If she was finally able in *Pointed Firs* to lift what she did know to the formal order of accomplished art, she earned the triumph by her single-minded devotion, through thirty years of work, to her narrow materials, the spare life and setting of the Maine coast, as much as by acquaintance with the outer world.[2] And as in her life she was both native and outlander, so through all her work runs a pattern of contrast between the in-world of the coastal villages, economically atrophied, and the bustling prosperous out-world from which the summer visitors come and into which the young, the active, the ambitious, invariably escape. To compare the initial full statement of this contrast in *Deephaven* with the more penetrating, and disturbing, intimations of *Pointed Firs,* twenty years after, gives a measure of her development as an artist.

---

[1]Preface to *Alexander's Bridge* (Boston, 1922), vii. The remark is quoted somewhat differently in *Not Under Forty* (New York, 1936), 88.

[2]F. O. Matthiessen, *Sarah Orne Jewett* (Boston, 1929), remains the best account of Jewett's personal experience of this region.

I

In *Deephaven* the summer visitors, two Boston girls, are the central figures, and the record of village life is the record of their self-consciously sensitive observation. They sympathize with the village in its evident decline into poverty and stagnation, and relish its lingering charm and beauty. But they are looking in from the outside. A positive class distinction between visitors and natives is all but asserted, and the visitors' patronizing approval, though well meant and not exactly offensive, is less attractive than Jewett seems to have realized. Similarly, though a part of her intention was clearly to pose, through the simple integrity of village manners, a pastoral criticism of the outer world, the fact that this criticism is delivered by outsiders, who will not stay, dissipates its force and leaves it vague and indecisive: "we told each other, as we went home in the moonlight down the quiet street, how much we had enjoyed the evening, for somehow [*sic*] the house and the people had nothing to do with the present, or the hurry of modern life."

In *Pointed Firs* the dispositions are altered. The emphasis is no longer divided, half on proving the observer's sensitivity. It is altogether on what she observes and apprehends—on the great presence of the natural landscape and on the figures in it who accept her into their community and tell her, enact before her, its almost buried life. Her sensitivity remains important in one respect only, that it opens the life of the village to her: her landlady, the herbgatherer Mrs. Todd, trusts her to keep shop; silent ruined men speak to her; she is allowed to be sympathetic with the "old ways"; and at the great tribal reunion which climaxes the book she may participate as an adopted member. But she never fully belongs, and there is no question of her staying. When she leaves in September, she must accept the rebuke implicit in Mrs. Todd's disinclination to stop for good-byes. The whole book has given an indelible impression of a community that is inexorably, however luminously, dying, but the narrator, as if to underscore what she is made to feel is a betrayal of privilege, of trust, now applies the metaphor of death not to the village but to herself:

> the little house had suddenly grown lonely, and my room looked
> empty as it had the day I came. I and all my belongings had died

out of it, and I knew how it would seem when Mrs. Todd came back
and found her lodger gone. So we die before our own eyes; so we
see some chapters of our lives come to their natural end.

The import of this, however, is equivocal: her departure is a
kind of dying but one which, precisely in departure, she can out-
live. And the final passage of *Pointed Firs,* though more simply
staged and less obviously eloquent than the affecting ending of
Deephaven, intensifies the ambiguity of feeling well beyond the
pathos and nostalgic allegiances of the earlier book. Sailing out of
the harbor and bay in early September, the narrator notices how
rain has made turf and woods green again, "like the beginning of
summer ashore"; and having thus established the still vital beauty
of the place, she looks back to see that "the islands and the head-
land had run together and Dunnet Landing and all its coasts
were lost to sight." The disappearance of the town into the landscape confirms its creeping decay; yet the beauty and vitality of
the setting asserts a superior fortune; and we cannot say whether
there is gain or loss in the departure, whether we are escaping
death or being cut off from some rare, transforming condition of
life.

What is notable here, in comparison with the ending of *Deephaven,* is both the greater emotional energy and also the greater
spareness, the concentration, the restrictive simplicity of statement. Less seems attempted, more actually is secured. The advance is strictly formal: the basic materials which compose the
Pointed Firs volume (1896) are all in *Deephaven* (1877) or in the
stories Jewett collected in *Tales of New England* (1894). No new
judgment is attempted, no different point of view arrived at. The
difference comes, on the one hand, in a mode of narration suited
as never before to the special nature of her apprehensions and,
on the other, in a simple sustaining structure within which she
could both elaborate and concentrate the thing she had to say.

It may be surprising, considering Jewett's reputation for crafts-
manship, to observe how little she had been able, up to *Pointed
Firs,* to master an art of narrative. She set, of course, high standards for herself: not the current fashion of local-color sketching
but the momentous example of *Madame Bovary* supported her
choice to write about "simple country people" and dwell upon
"trivialities and commonplaces in life."[3] She matured as a writer

in the shadow of Howells and Henry James, and measured herself, as they did, against the nineteenth-century European masters. The new lesson of realism, truthfulness of observation and rendering, was what she started from. The weakness in her early work is of another order—and I am not thinking simply of the patchiness of *Deephaven* (which was pieced together from magazine sketches). Her stories, even the most accomplished, are deficient precisely as stories; she simply does not manage narrative well. Her most scrupulous fidelity of observation, her most exactly suggestive delineation, cannot conceal and tend rather to underline the clumsiness and contrivance of the action. Sequences of unconvincing fantasy ("A White Heron"), coincidences and fatalities unsupported by a Hardy's positive intuition ("A Lost Lover"), clichés of melodrama ("Marsh Rosemary"), are what carry her stories along, from each carefully rendered situation to the next. It might be argued that she studied too exclusively the sentence of Flaubert which she kept pinned to her workdesk: "Ecrire la vie ordinaire comme on écrit l'histoire."[4] She might better have taken note of Mark Twain's "How to Tell a Story." The suggestion is not made facetiously; the mode of narrative Jewett did finally come around to in *Pointed Firs* is much closer to that celebrated by Mark Twain (and stock-in-trade with a host of regional yarn-spinners, journalists and entertainers, apprenticed like Twain to a thoroughly artful popular tradition) than to the technique of Flaubert or Henry James. The first-person narrator in *Pointed Firs* tells no stories herself; rather, she sets down stories which are told to her. And much of their "meaning," in fact, is in the struggle of the teller, himself participant, to do justice to the thing he has to tell; and their truth is confirmed in the wavering rhythm of his effort to express himself as his story seems to require. It is in these stories-within-the-story that the major themes of the book are most fully registered; the narrator's part is simply to describe the teller and the situation, to provide the occasion, to give notice of the passing of time—and, at the beginning and end of the book, to lead the reader sympathetically into the legended world of Dunnet Landing and safely, if equivocally, out again when the time comes. Jewett, it might be said,

[3]*Letters of Sarah Orne Jewett,* edited by Annie Fields (Boston, 1911), 82.
[4]*Ibid.,* 165.

solved her inability to master a Jamesian art of the short story by abandoning it.

Or she apprehended at last that what she had to tell was one story and one story only, one that all the earlier ones lead up to or provide analogies for. Another way of describing the achievement of *Pointed Firs* is to say, in these terms, that she had finally discovered within her materials—anecdotes, incident, scenes, special cases—the essential legend that was there for her to tell, and found for it an appropriate form. The lineaments of this legend are set down all through her earlier work (and in her letters), and it may be appropriate at this point to describe them, before going on to describe the structure she set them into in *Pointed Firs*.

II

The great event determining all others—rarely treated directly but persistently there as a shaping pressure—is the economic disintegration of the coastal towns, the withering away of the enterprise that gave them life. These towns, unlike the up-country farms and villages more characteristic of the work of Mrs. Stowe and Mrs. Freeman, did once belong to the great world of affairs and owned an oceanic vitality and breadth of prospect.[5] "Since the Embargo" hangs over Jewett's work like "before the War" over chronicles of the South. There remains no practicable future, and no promise in the present: "all the clocks in Deephaven, and all the people with them, had stopped years ago," and a sandbar fills the harbor mouth. The personal and family energy that went into commerce and community affairs now is spent in nostalgia and regret, in the breeding of "characters," or—as with Yeats's Sligo peasants and fishermen—in the cultivation of visions and voices; when the world of enterprise is sealed off, what remains for restless minds but the development of unmarketable psychic powers?[6] All the signs, though picturesque in themselves, betray

---

[5] A number of Jewett's sketches are set in country villages and farms, but the sea and its harbors and opportunities are almost always there in the background. If only as an outlet, an enlargement of prospect, vanished into the past perhaps but still haunting the present.

[6] See the chapter "Cunner Fishing" in *Deephaven*. In Yeats's *Reveries of*

the steady retreat into backwater stagnation. The wharves rot, the warehouses fall apart; and though the cottages and their kitchens, cupboards, and flowered borders are kept spruce and trim, they are lived in and tended by the old, the retired, the widowed, the unmarrying, the sick, the mad, the "uncompanioned."

The people of the region are its strictest measure—and still another sign of the perfection of Jewett's utterance in *Pointed Firs* is her concentration on persons, her resistance to distracting details. Landscape and local custom, the anonymous picturesque, are strongly present but now in the background; the burden of meaning is carried by specific personal histories. The types of character she worked with would not have been unfamiliar to her readers. It is a commonplace concerning the later New England local-color writing that young people rarely figure in it—few children, almost no young men, even more rarely an ordinary young couple. In *Deephaven* an unusual passage of open satire describes an evening lecture on "Elements of True Manhood," an inspirational discourse "directed entirely toward young men, and there was not a young man there." Young men of energy and promise are sure to be from the outside, like the young hunter of "A White Heron"—and are likely to represent a certain coarseness, a positive danger to the delicate balance of backwater life. For the home-grown the one remaining hope of manhood is to break away into the great world—again with the imputation, usually, of coarseness and self-ruination, as with the "lost lover" of Miss Horatia Dane. Those who stay are the weak and pathetic, the half-men, shiftless and full of "meechin' talk" like Jerry Lane of "Marsh Rosemary," whose "many years" older wife knows herself to be "the better man of the two."

"Ef *I* was a man..." she snaps at him contemptuously—and despairingly. There is no more striking symptom of the blight that has settled on the region that the recasting of customary social rôles, particularly of the roles of the sexes. The superiority of Jewett's work in the local-color genre—and here, too, *Pointed*

Childhood and Youth—with its references to the time of Galway's prosperity in commerce with Spain—there is a corresponding evocation of bygone economic rigor and the pathos of its passing, and of the warp and eccentricity that set in by default. The histories of the small ports along the Maine and Maritimes coast and that of a town like Sligo have more than a little in common.

Firs marks for her a distinct advance—appears in the combined
bluntness and subtlety, the overwhelming indirection, with which
she presents a norm of distorted, repressed, unfulfilled or transformed sexuality as an index to her essential story. When there is
a marriage, it is like that of Ann Floyd and Jerry Lane—the weak
boy marrying for protection and security the energetic spinster
who has the competence and strength of a proper man; that the
marriage is childless and ends in desertion does not come as a
surprise. More usually there is no marriage at all, simply the desertion, as in "A Lost Lover": here the elderly heroine, whose
lover was long ago supposed lost at sea but really has run away,
has come to be regarded as a widow and, on the basis of this lie,
a person of consequence in the village as well as in her own eyes;
she has achieved position and respect, but at the cost of playing a
woman's full part. The men do have the choice to go, though it
may destroy them, and only the already defeated or crippled,
the childish or woman-like, stay on. But for the women the only
choice, the sacrifice required for survival, is to give up a woman's
proper life and cover the default of the men, to be the guardians
and preservers of a community with no other source of vitality
and support. In a society without a future the woman's instinct to
carry on the life of the tribe can only be fulfilled by devotion to
what remains, and her energies must go to preservation of the
past, to intercourse with nature, to disguising and delaying the
inevitable dissolution. This is the ambiance even of a story like
"A White Heron," in which the heroine is only a little girl. In
the presence of the hunter "the woman's heart, asleep in the
child," stirs with a premonition of the power and release of love;
but in defense of her mysterious sympathy with wild creatures
and her secret knowledge of the heron's sanctuary, she refuses
his appeal like a profaning courtship (in his offering her money
there is again the imputation of grossness); and the suggestion is
made that her whole life will turn on this renunciation.

    The story of the region, we may say, would not be honestly told
if the sexual warping were not brought into it, but it would not
be fully told if that were made the main, the climactic, theme of it.
Sexuality figures, rather, as one among several of the great natural
contingencies determining the forms life must take in this life-
abandoned society. Old age and death are another: it is with the
aged that the pressure of decay is registered most vividly. Ex-

ternal nature provides the others—thus, perhaps, in the final clarifying of her vision and refining of its expression, Jewett's choice of title; and thus, in *The Country of the Pointed Firs,* the constant counterpointing of personal and tribal histories by the invoked presence not only of the landscape but of season and weather, too, and the incessant audible movement of the sea in its storms and calms, its tidal rise and fall.[7] Only society is dying, only *human* life: water, rock, woods, birds, vegetation are alive and—in the time we are allowed to look at them—surpassingly beautiful. The season is nearly always early or full summer, and rarely later than the first touch of fall; it is as though winter, re-inforcing all too harshly the testimony of the region's economic life, were too terrible to contemplate.

Framed by the vitality of the landscape and the inanition of human affairs, a fight for life goes on through all Jewett's work. The sexual warping is subsumed by this more general tension between the signs of natural power and the signs of impotence and death. In *Deephaven* the one show of "business-like" community life is for a funeral. Ironically the dead man is to the mourners a figure of awe and envy rather than of regret; he is "immeasurably their superior now. Living, he had been a failure...but now, if he could come back, he would know secrets, and be wise beyond anything they could imagine, and who could know the riches of which he might have come into possession?" The circumstances of life are such that one must either covet death or (like courteous, bewildered, mad Miss Chauncey in perhaps the best single chapter of *Deephaven*) "disbelieve" in it. The struggle to delay extinction appears, in Jewett's people, exhausting. Human life cannot survive in its customary forms and must be absorbed into the timeless cycles of nature. And even nature may be ambiguous. Even summer is not to be trusted. There is an "early summer-tiredness that belongs to New Englanders of the old stock," Sarah Jewett wrote to Sara Norton in 1898.[8] Summer she described ("The Courting of Sister Wisby") as the season which to the New Englander "must always last," must become permanent; that it does not, her own birthday came the 3rd of September to remind

---

[7]It is remarkable how near the book comes to the literary naturalist vision of life as being pathetically determined by great impersonal and uncontrollable forces in nature and society.

[8]*Letters,* 146.

her. And in the opening paragraphs of "Sister Wisby," set in
late August, she expressed the grievous ephemerality of the upper
New England summer with a positively Hawthornean appre-
hension: under the "cool cloak of bracing air,"

> Every living thing grows suddenly cheerful and strong; it is only
> when you catch sight of a horror-stricken little maple in swampy
> soil,—a little maple that has second sight and foreknowledge of
> coming disaster to her race,—only then does a distrust of autumn's
> friendliness dim your joyful satisfaction.

So *Deephaven* ends in falling leaves and bleak autumn days—
though perversely, at the moment of departure, the sun is out
again and Indian summer beginning: "we wished that it had
been a rainy day." Even in the finest weather the tide will ebb and
the sea turn rough—though in the closing sentence of *Deephaven* it is imagined moving and speaking "lazily in its idle, high-
tide sleep."

III

Some aspects of the structure of *Pointed Firs,* the definitive
order Jewett here devised for her materials, have already been
mentioned.[9] There is the main sequence of action and of time—
as the book ends with the narrator's departure in early fall, it

[9]The text I have used in this analysis is that of the first edition (1896). Jewett
wrote additional Dunnet Landing stories which have been incorporated into
later editions, though not during her lifetime and not, apparently, by her
authorization; thus, Cather's edition of 1925 and the Doubleday Anchor edition
(1956) include three sketches (chs. 21-23) not in the original book. Two of these,
"The Queen's Twin" and "A Dunnet Shepherdess," were first published in a
separate collection, *The Queen's Twin and Other Stories* (1899). In a 1910 re-
printing of several volumes (copyright Mary R. Jewett) "A Dunnet Shepherdess"
and "William's Wedding" were added to *Pointed Firs;* "The Queen's Twin" was
still printed separately. Cather's edition was the first to lodge all three of these
within the text of *Pointed Firs* (her preface acknowledges that "William's Wedding" was "uncompleted at the time of Miss Jewett's death").

I mention all this to explain why I have gone back to the first edition as the
proper text. Also, though the three subsequently added chapters are competent-
ly performed, they seem to me the least bit arch and over-explanatory, and they
definitely interrupt—coming as they now do just before the closing chapter—
the poignant falling rhythm of the original work.

opens with her arrival in June and moves through the phases of a summer. And there is the steady counterpointing of human undertakings with the natural setting—a pattern of notation which appears on nearly every page. Spelling this out in full detail, however, would be impractical and not really very helpful, since we would still have to identify the art that keeps it from lapsing into pathetic fallacy; also, this is the part of Jewett's craft which she mastered first and which therefore will not in itself account for the superiority of *Pointed Firs*. It is enough to say that her observation of setting—of the changes of sea and sky, the colors of the landscape and the old buildings, the variety of scenes and view—being accurate and economical is always convincing, and moreover is never used to claim for the immediate situation a feeling or an implication not already established in the human sphere; it fills naturally the pauses which mark the passing of time in a place with so much time on its hands.

The principal ordering device is no more complicated or esoteric than those so far spoken of, and has the bold simplicity that only an artist free of uncertainty or embarrassment about her material would think to rely on—it is simply the arrangement of chapters and of episodes. The twenty-one chapters of *Pointed Firs* fall into six distinct groupings; between the brief opening and closing sequences there are four central episodes which form the body of the book. Each has, within a scaled-down minimum of incident, its distinguishing quality of feeling and its particular scope of suggestion; and their arrangement, though perfectly casual, does not seem indeliberate.

The first three chapters form the opening section and are used chiefly to get the narrator established in Dunnet Landing and in her own role there. She arrives, she introduces Mrs. Todd, she settles on a vacant hill-top schoolhouse as her place of work. Nothing more has happened, though in a few phrases some of the main themes have been announced—in the "mixture of remoteness, and childish certainty of being the centre of civilization," which is her first stated impression of the atmosphere of the village, its whole actual history is suggested; in the few sentences on Mrs. Todd's practice of the mysteries of herb-lore we are given a first mild symbol of the devices human energy is put to merely to survive in this place; and in the story Mrs. Todd tells the narrator, as intimacy grows between them, of the man she had loved as a girl but could not marry, we are put in touch with the primary myth so many of Jewett's stories of this region make use of—of the man who went out into the world and the woman who stayed behind.

The next three chapters (iv-vi) carry the first of the four main episodes, which centers on Captain Littlepage and the story he has to tell. He is seen first at a funeral (which furnishes in a few lines a paradigm of all the counterpointing of people and place— the "futile and helpless" procession winding along the rocky shore under the "clear, high sky" of "a glorious day early in July"), a mysterious figure, aged and worn, "the one strange and unrelated person in all the company." He comes then to the schoolhouse, and as he talks, quoting Milton and Shakespeare and speaking of the old days and the old stock, we are shown a character of intelligence and refinement from which the original strength and air of command have not quite entirely disappeared. It is he who most bluntly points the contrast between past and present, between the lifeless provincial isolation of the village now and the days when its men, and their wives and children, too, "saw the world for themselves" and "were some acquainted with foreign lands an' their laws." And it is he who declares the plain bitter truth which all the gentleness and sympathy of the narration cannot mitigate, that it is "low water mark now here in Dunnet," and that "there's nothing to take the place of shipping in a place like ours." "There's no large-minded way of thinking now," his lament goes on, and though coming out of the narrowest of circumstances, rises in its own colloquial voice to some of the turns of phrase, even something of the manner of judgment, of Yeats's oracular "Second Coming": "the worst have got to be best and rule everything; we're all turned upside down and going back year by year." It is Yeats's vision of chaos particularized, given a local history and habitation.

Yet the story Littlepage tells has the curious effect of ratifying this disaster he complains of, this drawing in of the village on itself. It is a tale of "strange events," of an encounter with the outer world so bewildering and terrific as to break a man's strength and wither his ambition. It is a tale within a tale, of a vision in uncharted northern waters of a great town peopled by ghostly forbidding human figures which glided out of sight when approached but attacked a boat's crew of men as they tried to get away. "A place where there was neither living nor dead," Captain Littlepage says, "a kind of waiting place between this world an' the next." In some ways this is the boldest and most decisive passage in the book, for it secures that reference to the life of male action and encounter without which the narrator's sympathy for backwater Dunnet would seem myopic, sentimental. It is simply an old man's hallucination, yet also a fable of the ungovernable anonymous forces which have closed the village off from life and the world. This fearful mid-world is what those who go out from a Dunnet Landing must enter; good reason then to choose to stay home—even though it must be to wither and stiffen in a setting which, in its mild and permissive way, is only another kind of mid-world, half way over to death.

Mrs. Todd has a rational explanation for Captain Littlepage's stories—too much reading has affected his mind. Yet the narrator makes a point of showing her disturbed by them, and at the beginning of the second of the four central episodes we are brought up short by the same metaphor: the sunlight falling on Green Island, where Mrs. Todd's mother lives heartily on, "like a sudden revelation of *the world beyond this* which some believe to be so near" (my italics). The analogy to Littlepage's city of ghosts seems unmistakable. Ultimately, in *Pointed Firs,* there is no disguising what sort of equivocal refuge from the onset of life and death even the loveliest sanctuary must provide.

But for the most part this second episode (chs. vii-xi) sounds a less troubled note. Here indeed we are made to feel most concentratedly the power of nature along this coast to sustain an equable degree of life. The action is of the simplest: on one of the fine mornings of early summer the narrator goes out to Green Island with Mrs. Todd for a day's visit. The loveliness of the island and the vivacity of its octogenarian mistress, Mrs. Blackett, set the tone for the idyll of these chapters. If Dunnet Landing is provincial and isolated, what must Green Island be, "so apparently neighborless and remote?" A world unto itself, the narrator says, "a complete and tiny continent," a place where "it was impossible not to wish to stay on forever," a retreat fostering "that final, that highest gift of heaven," that "perfect self-forgetfulness" which is the secret of Mrs. Blackett's power of survival. The pasturage is thin but sweet; there are wild flowers and shrubs, sheep and fishing weirs, and the solid, immaculate, hospitable house with its unused best parlor and sociable kitchen; and from the height of land (in the climactic passage closing chapter ix) a grand view opens out over the whole coast: "It gave a sudden sense of space, for nothing stopped the eye or hedged one in,— that sense of liberty in space and time which great prospects always give."

Life and space, an unconstricted prospect—these are the notes sounded in the Green Island chapters. The opposing conditions are not forgotten, and are to have their due soon enough; here, however, they are softened, and serve to make what is to be valued at Green Island the more attractive. Treated differently, Mrs. Blackett's son William—the childlike man of sixty whose mother must still speak for him in company—could have been used to overset all that is claimed through the old mother and her snug retreat; instead, Jewett is concerned to give in William the the image of a life which, far from having been wasted by its circumstances, has found its only possible security there. The one positively disquieting note is in the story Mrs. Todd is moved to tell, being caught off guard by the recovered charm of the place, of her courtship and marriage long ago—of her inability to love her honest husband as she was loved, of his death at sea and the long widowhood in which their marriage has come to be no more than a dream to her. So even in this sanctuary of life and space, death and time intrude, in deprivations and constrained adjustments.[10] But at the end of the episode the narrator comes back to the wide view from Mrs. Blackett's bedroom, a "place of peace" and "quiet outlook upon field and sea and sky," and to the pungent savor of the herb-garden mixing with the sea-wind—the signs of an ineradicable vitality.

The next section exactly reverses the major and minor themes of the Green Island sequence—in this counter-idyll death and time are made the keynotes, and life and spaciousness are seen to belong only to the indifferent presences of nature. Significantly we are brought forward in these chapters (xii-xv) into dry August, beyond the freshness of early summer. Again there is a

[10]Just here we have the well-known image of Mrs. Todd as an "Antigone alone on the Theban plain," possessed by "an absolute, archaic grief" in the contemplation of unfulfilled tribal pieties and duties—a figure often praised but more for verifying the classic seriousness of Jewett's art than for its obvious appropriateness to her broad theme.

story recalled from older times—the stage being set in the intermediate twelfth chapter as the narrator listens to Mrs. Todd and her visitor Mrs. Fosdick tolling the past, recording the lives and the changes, deaths without entrances. Their story is of "poor Joanna," and like the preceding episode has its corroborative setting to point the contrast—this is Shell-heap Island, a forbidding, barely accessible place with "a different look from any of the other islands," and the object, with its Indian relics, of much local superstition and legend: "a dreadful small place to make a world of." Here in solitude lived Joanna Todd, "a sort of a nun or hermit person"—and as Captain Littlepage's story may be taken as a parable of a man's options in this country, Joanna's is an archetype of the woman's. Here is the region's primary fable, of the girl "full o' feeling" who lost her man to the outer world and whose life was closed off before it had begun; in her desolation she put off alone for Shell-heap Island and never returned. The rising tempo of the old women's recollection is deftly used to establish the gravity of the story. At first reluctant to tell it out, Mrs. Todd soon takes it up with the absorption and unselfconsciousness of a ritual performance. She had been one of the first to see Joanna after her withdrawal out of the world; and one of [the—Ed.] freighted climaxes of the book comes in Mrs. Todd's account of how, after a blundering minister had spoken in his cold word, she caught up Joanna in her arms and begged her to come back into life with her, Joanna's refusal, her conviction that she had "committed the unpardonable sin" ("We don't seem to hear nothing about that now," Mrs. Fosdick remarks), is like the obsession of Captain Littlepage, pitiable perhaps but not lacking nobility. Without ignoring anything of the eccentricity and barrenness of these lives, Jewett succeeded in *Pointed Firs* in heightening them, not to tragedy exactly, but to a moving solemnity, confirming as by a pageant, a *tableau vivant*, their impersonal necessity and their vulnerability, despite all show of endurance, to time and death.

As before, a balance is kept in this episode between the contrasting themes. So Joanna's utter "loneliness of sorrow" comes to us through Mrs. Todd's robust compassion. So, too, in a coda to her story, in which the narrator pays her own visit to Shell-heap Island, time and death, though not denied authority over life, are briefly displaced as the sheer physical presence of the island brings Joanna's story to life in the narrator's imagination; and in a final passage that recalls the eloquent last paragraph of chapter 58 of *Moby Dick,* Joanna's life is presented as no more than the familiar norm of our human condition: "In the life of each of us... there is a place remote and islanded, and given to endless regret or secret happiness; we are each the uncompanioned hermit and recluse of an hour or a day; we understand our fellows of the cell to whatever age of history they may belong."

One more main episode remains, as the season now draws on to an end. Again the keynote is changed; now the stress is back on the sedulous human bustle and not, for a time, on its constriction and fatality. This is the Bowden family reunion, plainly symbolic, on which virtually the whole population of the region converges as if to renew its stubborn hold on life. There is room now for relaxations of humor, for *genre* comedy, as the clans gather and their "characters" go on display—the doctor's rivalry with Mrs. Todd's herb practice, Cousin Sant Bowden's military drill-mastering, the huddling over family resemblances, and so on. But the cheerfulness and bustle speak for deeper qualities, too, and the narrator is prompt to interpret them: they indicate "the hidden fire of enthusiasm" which is not yet gone out of the New England nature but, "once given an outlet...shines forth with almost volcanic light and heat," breaking through "the granite dust in which our souls are set." The "transfiguring powers" we are asked to credit to this occasion are verified in the narrator's account of the solemn slow procession into the waterside picnic grove, moving for all the world, she observes, like a company of pagans going out to worship some "god of harvests":

> It was strangely moving to see this and to make part of it. The sky, the sea, have watched poor humanity at its rites so long; we were no more a New England family celebrating its own existence and simple progress; we carried the tokens and inheritance of all such households from which this had descended, and were only the latest of our line. We possessed the instincts of a far, forgotten childhood; I found myself thinking that we ought to be carrying green branches and singing as we went.

A focal passage, clearly—and though the reunion trails off into crotchety gossip and frayed tempers, its weight of suggestion carries through. For once, before straggling back to their isolated individual struggles merely to endure, these people have acted together as a living community and asserted their life as a continuing race. Against "the waste of human ability in this world" which their lives betray, they have made at least a show of the "reserve force of society."

After this, the common fate having been conspired against by this ritual of postponement, the narrator may take her leave. But the end of the book is not quite yet. If I am insisting on the deliberateness of form in *Pointed Firs,* I do not mean that it is rigidly or arithmetically calculated. There is one more chapter (xx), before the last, that does not belong to any particular phase of the summer, as do the various main episodes, and that does not take in charge one particular concentration of feeling. It begins as little more than a character sketch; indeed the first rendering of Elijah Tilley ("such an evasive, discouraged-looking person, heavy-headed and stooping," chirping in suitable dialect about "haddick" and baked potatoes) seems mildly condescending like nothing else in the narrative so far. But as it moves into Mr. Tilley's house and the open-hearted flow of his talk, the dignity of an unobtrusive pathos is resumed, and we are given a summary image of the equivocal devisings life has came to in this place. He is one of the last survivors of the old time, one whose mind now seems "fixed upon nature and the elements rather than upon any contrivances of man." Like Mrs. Todd and Mrs. Blackett, Littlepage and Joanna, he has found his own way of holding on against the ebbing of the old vitality. His life, however, is different in one respect from all the others, in being wholly devoted, quite unreconciled, to the lost forms of human society that once sustained it. His main energy and skill go to serving the memory of his dead wife and keeping up their house as she left it—knitting, mending, making shift, missing her without abatement, and talking of nothing else. His recital becomes an elegy not only for the dead woman and for their life together, but for all the lives and households in the country of the pointed firs, by this old man who has come to be both wife and husband in his house (as William Blackett is both son and daughter in his) and by this shift has forestalled to the limit of his capacity the ruinous work of time—a "ploddin' man," as Mrs. Todd must say of him, but also, through the entirety of his absorption, a transfigured one. A final image of Mrs. Todd, in the short last chapter, catches up the implication of Mr. Tilley's manner of life and indeed of all the personal histories which Jewett's book is constructed from—we see her as a figure "mateless and appealing," yet "strangely self-possessed."

IV

All form is "significant"—but some forms (to borrow a cadence) are more significant than others. A demonstration of structural wholeness does not prove, nor does it explain, the impressiveness of a piece of writing. Examining structure, we find ourselves judging substance and implication as well—and no doubt operating from pre-judgments (usually unspoken though not necessarily not understood) as to interest and worth. There is nothing illegitimate in this. How else do we identify the specific gravity and bearing, the importance, of a work? We judge certain perceptions more commanding than others; we scarcely bother to *raise* questions of art or the lack of it unless our serious attention is commanded.

What is it then in Jewett's *Pointed Firs* that does so command attention, that secures the impression not only of integrity but of significance (and so of the durability Willa Cather claimed for it)? The book, we observe, proceeds through a sequence of personal histories and personal encounters. Yet the specific events, one by one, are too slight to produce much more than anecdotal pathos; what gives them body and interest is their insistent revelation of a more general order of existence. Particular persons have been put sharply before us, yet our feeling for their lives, though warm enough, is curiously impersonal; our interest in them is less as personalities than as examples, as case histories.

In this respect *Pointed Firs* is no special case. In most of the best "local-color" writing, as even in more ambitious work like Anderson's *Winesburg,* the interest in character is negligible— that is, as "character" is properly understood in fiction: persons moved through a convincing range of human response to moral decision or commitment. Instead there is an interest in line-drawing, or in caricature—a sociological interest, essentially. If *Pointed Firs* is exceptional as a work of art, it is so only through perfection of its *genre;* in substance and implication it is sociological, and historical. The powerful compulsions of American

democratic life have always been too ambiguous and diverse—
and too relentlessly novel—to be easily registered or immediately
identified; what the restricted focus of "regionalism" has provided in our literature is a way of bringing them to expression
and putting them in some sort of objective judgment. So a great
part of what holds us to a *Pointed Firs* or a *Winesburg* is the
clarity and accuracy of their testimony as to the experience of
these compulsions and urgencies which in our civilization have
traditionally worked (so witnesses as different as Tocqueville and
Poe, Mark Twain and Henry Adams, Jewett and Anderson, have
told us) to sap private morals, obliterate individuality, and transform persons into grotesque national phenomena.

To say then that *Pointed Firs* is a masterpiece of the local-color
school (its only peer would seem to be "Old Times on the Mississippi") is not at all to talk it down. The work of this school, the
bulk of it produced between 1870 and 1900, constitutes a poten-
tially powerful criticism of the main directions of American life.
Set sometimes in the past and recalled from the perspective of a
transformed present, and sometimes in some backwater of the
present seen from the turbulent main stream, these books hold up
for inspection (occasionally satirical, more often affectionate and
elegiac) some local pattern of community life which has already
vanished or is on the point of vanishing and which in its isolation and decay gives off a luminous but pathetic (if not terrible)
beauty—the flush of dying. These are the jolly corners of American life (Henry James, not equipped to look in the usual places,
found them at Washington Square as well), and in the best of the
literature that celebrates them there is not only a compassionate
response to their ill fortune but also a knowledgeable criticism of
what has overtaken them; in the very best the criticism returns
upon the region itself—the jolly corner proves to be appalling,
deadly, maleficent—and we find expressed a fatalism beyond
nostalgia or irony, a sense of American life as requiring, as being
founded upon, the pitiless extinction of the past, the violent ex-
tirpation of amenity and beauty and of every temporary establish-
ment of that truly civil order which is the earliest of American
dreams.[11]

[11]It does not seem accidental that the fashion of local-color writing should
have coincided with the hey-day of populism and the beginnings of muckrake
journalism. All responded to the same kind of intuition about American society;

The art of *Pointed Firs* reaches this order of revelation—a rare enough achievement. The very conditions in our civilization which provoke such books and such judgments seem to act also to deprive them of body and cogency. Instead of an intelligible and practicable criticism what we are likely to get from even our most conscientious talents is self-pity and hysteria. Performances and lives which in England, under similar provocation, have traditionally turned eccentric yet still can make themselves felt along the central axis, have tended rather in our centerless country to fly off the handle altogether. An hysterical assertion of special fears and delusions, and of special privileges and immunities from the main course of our democratic, technological, acquisitive society underlies more than just our local-color writing. Not only New England spinsters but national dignitaries —statesmen, evangelists, bankers, editors of great newspapers, men of letters and scholarship—are driven to nostalgic fantasy, and yearn for imaginary pasts with a violence matched only by their will to overlook the real one. The claiming of permanence and sovereign value for the most obviously adventitious and unsavory conditions is the national disease of what more than one of our writers has divined to be a nation of (though perhaps never more than half-deliberate) confidence men. Is there one among our significant writers whose very life has not been a self-conscious, energy-consuming struggle to get and stay on some sort of center without going dead? Is there one of our classic books which is not in good part a critique of this hysteria, an exposure of these false parturitions of the spirit and of the civilization that compulsively generates them? Ours is a literature that springs, when it springs at all, from violent contradictions of idealized feeling, that makes a specialty of sudden fruition and melancholy aftermaths, that knows—with ambiguous exceptions like Henry James—no middle ground between extraordinary originality and equally extraordinary tastelessness, self-imitation, banality. A pragmatical literature, we might call it—one rarely able to live

---

and as the populists and muckrakers pointed an actively accusing, reformist finger at what industrial, metropolitan, corporate society was getting the country into, the local colorists, accusing passively through a submissive nostalgia, projected images of what the country was being led away from; frequently there was pooling of effort, as in Mrs. Freeman's *The Portion of Labor* or Lincoln Steffens's charming account of his California childhood.

(and this is a source of strength as well as a limitation) except in immediate contact with its undistilled and unprinted sources of feeling. So all but a few of its finest books, and *Pointed Firs* is a perfect instance, ground their strength and appeal, and find their form, not in some objective order of thought or judgment but in a tenuous *ad hoc* balancing of intense and contradictory emotion — a balance or tension which, as it can give surprising authority to a style like Jewett's that otherwise follows a conventional rhetoric, requires in the first place a rare artfulness to get control of and maintain; which may achieve for the space of a single work the creating and sustaining force of some deep-grounded formal idea, yet will barely submit to argument or rational analysis.

Jewett's ultimate art in *Pointed Firs* is to sustain this creative balance of crossed feelings — to make for her materials a claim of value and permanence but to show it as hopeless. Readers of her letters and other work know that she was not free of certain "hysterias" of her time and society.[12] Her judgments of present and past antedated her proving them in her art. But prove them she did — by making them as impersonal as the sympathy we are brought to feel for her characters; by suffusing them with the durable colors of legend, the solemnity of history. *The Country of the Pointed Firs* is a small work but an unimprovable one, with a secure and unrivaled place in the main line of American literary expression.

[12]See Ferman Bishop, "Sarah Orne Jewett's Ideas of Race," *New England Quarterly,* XXX (June 1957), 243-249.

Introduction to *The Collected Short Stories of Edith Wharton*

by R. W. B. Lewis

I

Edith Wharton began as a writer of short stories and, in a sense, she finished as one. Her first publications (apart from the poems that appeared anonymously in the New York *World* and the *Atlantic Monthly,* and were privately printed as *Verses* in 1878) were a series of stories brought out by *Scribner's,* starting with the issue of July, 1891, when Mrs. Wharton was in her thirtieth year. By the time she completed her first novel, *The Valley of Decision,* in 1902, two volumes of her shorter works has appeared, volumes which included such fine and remarkably varied stories as "A Journey," "The Pelican," "Souls Belated" and "The Recovery." And while she wrote no unquestionably first-rate full-length novel after *The Age of Innocence* in 1920 — *The Buccaneers,* had she lived to finish and revise it, might have proved the gratifying exception — the four collections of stories in those later years contained items as distinguished as "A Bottle of Perrier," "After Holbein," "Roman Fever" and "All Souls'," the latter composed apparently within a year or so of her death in 1937. Mrs. Wharton produced eighty-six stories in all, leaving behind in addition several promising but tantalizing fragmentary manuscripts; and of this impressive number, eighteen or twenty strike this reader as very good indeed, many more as displaying an at least occasional excellence (the description of an Italian garden, the disclosure of a moral quirk, a flash of wit), and no one of them as totally bereft of interest.

What does distinguish the best of them must be specified with some care. It cannot be said, for example, that Mrs. Wharton significantly modified the genre itself—as during her lifetime, James Joyce and D. H. Lawrence and Ernest Hemingway were so differently doing. On the formal side, she was, to borrow a phrase from Louis Auchincloss, "a caretaker." She was the dedicated preserver of classical form in narrative, of the orderly progression in time and the carefully managed emphasis which, she reminds us in "Telling a Short Story," the French writers of *contes* had derived from the Latin tradition and the English in turn had taken over from the French. In "Telling a Short Story" (the second chapter of her book, *The Writing of Fiction,* 1925), Mrs. Wharton says much that is engrossing and valid, but virtually nothing that is new, at least to a reader of late Victorian literature. Perhaps the one surprising element—I shall come back to this—is her special admiration for the ghost story, "the peculiar category of the eerie" to which she turns her attention at once, even before getting down to questions about subject matter, characterization and the proper degree of economy in the short story proper. Elsewhere, she talks sensibly about "unity of vision," the strategically chosen "register" or point of view by which the experience is to be seen and by which it is to be shaped, with due acknowledgment to Henry James for first establishing the primacy of this fictional resource. She observes that the development and exploration of character is not the business of the short story, but rather that of the novel. And she lays it down that "situation is the main concern of the short story," so that "the effect produced by the short story depends entirely on its form, or presentation."

Such critical language does not sound very demanding, and in story after story Mrs. Wharton remained faithful to the principles announced. An old lady's view of the grubby yards adjacent to her boardinghouse—her one consolation in life—is about to be cut off; a young woman returning from Colorado to New York with her desperately sick husband, finds that he is lying dead in his sleeping-car berth and that she may be put off the train, with his corpse, in the midst of nowhere; a married woman has fled to Italy with her lover; a young man who is about to be exposed as an embezzler prepares to escape to Canada—in each case, we are introduced at once to a "situation." And yet in practice, Edith

Wharton was often subtler, and both her ambition and her imaginative achievement greater, than her common sense critical remarks might lead one to expect.

Early stories like "That Good May Come" and "A Cup of Cold Water" do in fact consist in the *working out* of a given situation, the active resolution, happily or unhappily, of some moral dilemma. But in the best of her stories—in "Souls Belated," "The Other Two," "The Eyes," "Autres Temps…," "A Bottle of Perrier" and others—it is rather that the situation itself is gradually revealed in all its complexity and finality. What we know at the end, in these "crucial instances," is not so much how some problem got resolved, but the full nature, usually the insurmountable nature, of the problem itself. It is then that Mrs. Wharton's stories gain the stature she attributed to the finest stories everywhere— those, in her account, which combined French form with Russian profundity: they become "a shaft driven straight into the heart of experience." It is then too that they comprise what she felt all so rightly any work of fiction should seek to comprise: a judgment on life, an appraisal of its limits, an assessment of the options—if options there be—that life has to offer. The immediate human situation has, in short, become a paradigm of the human condition.

II

The situations she chose so to treat and to enlarge upon are not, at first glance, very original or unusual ones. In "Telling a Short Story," Mrs. Wharton quotes with approval Goethe's contention that "those who remain imprisoned in the false notion of their own originality will always fall short of what they might have accomplished." Mrs. Wharton, who entertained no such false notion, was content with the received forms and conventions of the short story; and she did not attempt to apply the art of storytelling to any hitherto unheard-of subject. There was, however, one area of experience which she was perhaps the first *American* writer to make almost exclusively her own: even more, I dare say, than Henry James, who would in any event be her only rival in this respect. This is what, in the loose groupings of stories appended to this introduction, I call the marriage question.

I have collected almost two dozen titles under this head, but the list could be much longer: several of those gathered under "Art and Human Nature" and nearly all those under "Ghosts" and "Romance and History" could be said to belong there as well. To point to so persistent a concern may seem only to stress the resolutely traditional cast of Mrs. Wharton's imagination; for while American fiction in the nineteenth century (before Howells and James) had not much focused on the marriage question, that question had provided the theme of themes for a whole galaxy of English, French and Russian writers. A generation for whom the marriage question tends to be sporadic and peripheral is likely to forget its former centrality, and to suppose that for Jane Austen, for Trollope, for Stendhal, for Tolstoi, the question was *merely* the occasion for some far more arresting human drama. And a generation that does so may find it difficult to appreciate how much Mrs. Wharton, examining the question over the years, managed to make of it.

She made, one might say, almost everything of it. It is not only that she explored so many phases and dimensions of the question: the very grounds for marrying, and premarital maneuvering, in "The Quicksand," "The Dilettante," "The Introducers" and others; the stresses and strains, the withering hopes and forced adjustments of the marital relation in "The Fullness of Life," "The Lamp of Psyche," "The Letters," "Diagnosis" and elsewhere; the intricate issue of divorce in "The Last Asset," "The Other Two," "Austres Temps…"; the emotional and psychological challenge of adultery in "Souls Belated," "Atrophy," "The Long Run," and so on; the phenomenon of illegitimacy in "Her Son," "Roman Fever" and with gentle mockery in "His Father's Son"; the ambiguous value of children in the piercingly satirical "The Mission of Jane." It is not only that her treatment of the question, in these multiple phases, displays so broad a range of tone and perspective, and so keen an eye for the dissolving and emergent structures of historical institutional and social life with which the question was enmeshed. It is that the question, as Mrs. Wharton reflected on it, dragged with it all the questions about human nature and conduct to which her generous imagination was responsive.

There are of course urgent biographical reasons for Edith Wharton's near obsession with the perplexities of marriage, though, as I shall suggest, her deeper and more private passions found covert expression in ghost stories and romances. The chief cluster of stories bearing upon marriage, divorce and adultery were written during the years (up to 1913) when her personal problems in those regards were most pressing: when, among other things, her own marriage was becoming unbearable to her, when her husband Edward Robbins ("Teddy") Wharton was succumbing to mental illness and given ever more frequently to bouts of disjointed irascibility, and when her relation to Walter Berry (the international lawyer who was her mentor and romantic idol) arrived at one peak of intensity. But whatever the immediate causes, the whole domain of the marriage question was the domain in which Edith Wharton sought the truth of human experience; it was where she tested the limits of human freedom and found the terms to define the human mystery.

"Souls Belated" is an excellent case in point. The situation there is that of Mrs. Lydia Tillotson, who has abandoned her husband and come to Europe with her lover Ralph Gannett to spend a year wandering through Italy and then to settle for a time, registered as man and wife, at a resort hotel on one of the Italian lakes. Her divorce decree is at this moment granted, and the lovers are free to marry; but Lydia, to Gannett's astonishment, is passionately opposed to remarrying. She is appalled at the thought of yielding to that conventional necessity, of returning to the social fold and eventually of being received by the very people she had hoped to escape. "You judge things too theoretically," Gannett tells her. "Life is made up of compromises." "The life we ran away from—yes!" she replies. To this Gannett remarks with a smile: "I didn't know that we ran away to found a new system of ethics. I supposed it was because we loved each other." One of the merits of "Souls Belated" is the author's delicate division of sympathy between Lydia's anguished impulse to escape and Gannett's readiness to compromise (just as one of this early story's minor flaws is a certain shiftiness in point of view); but it is evident that on this occasion Gannett speaks for Edith Wharton. The impossibility of founding a new ethic—of a man and woman arranging their life together on a new and socially unconventional basis—was one of Mrs. Wharton's most somber convictions, and a conviction all the stronger because (partly out of her own anguish) she tested it again and again in her stories.

Edith Wharton's moral imagination, as it exercised itself on this fundamental theme, may be usefully contrasted with that of D. H. Lawrence. Writing about Anna Karenina and Vronsky (in his posthumously published *Study of Thomas Hardy*), Lawrence argued that, in effect, Tolstoi had let his characters down; that "their real tragedy is that they are unfaithful to the greater unwritten morality" (greater, that is, than conventional social morality), "which would have bidden Anna be patient and wait until she, by virtue of greater right, could take what she needed from society; would have bidden Vronsky detach himself from the system, become an individual, creating a new colony of morality with Anna." In *Women in Love* and *Lady Chatterley's Lover,* Lawrence presents us with couples who do detach themselves from the system and do seek to create just such a new colony. Neither Birkin and Ursula nor Connie Chatterley and Mellors meet with much success; the site of the new colony is not located within the bounds of the two novels. But given Lawrence's apocalyptic view of modern industrial society, and his intense belief that no genuine human relation can be consummated within it, it is the continuing search that Lawrence espoused.

For Edith Wharton, the effort was utterly doomed from the start; society, crushing as it might be, was all there was. "I want to get away with you," Newland Archer tells Ellen Olenska in *The Age of Innocence,* "into a world...where we shall be simply two human beings who love each other, who are the whole of life to each other." Mme. Olenska's reply is poignant and final. "Oh my dear—where is that country? Have you ever been there?" So it is in "Souls Belated": Lydia tries to leave Gannett, but she knows she has literally no place to go; she comes wearily back to him, and at the story's end they are heading for Paris and the ceremony which will marry them back into respectable society.

The relation between man and woman—whether marital or extramarital—was, in Mrs. Wharton's sense of it, beset by the most painful contradictions. "I begin to see what marriage is for," Lydia Tillotson says in "Souls Belated." "It's to keep people away from each other. Some times I think that two people who love each other can be saved from madness only by the things that come between them—children, duties, visits, bores, relations.... Our sin," she ends up, is that "we've seen the nakedness of each other's souls." But such dire proximity, such exposed nakedness—which

Mrs. Wharton seems to have ardently desired and fearfully shrunk from—could occur within marriage as well.

Her consciousness of the dilemma was made evident in the exchange that took place a good many years after the writing of "Souls Belated" between Mrs. Wharton and Charles Du Bos, the gifted French essayist and student of French and English literature, who had known her since 1905, when he undertook to translate *The House of Mirth.* On an afternoon in the summer of 1912, driving through the French countryside, the two of them had been comparing their favorite literary treatments of married life. In fiction, they agreed upon George Eliot's *Middlemarch,* and Du Bos quoted the words of the heroine, Dorothea Brooke, that "marriage is so unlike anything else—there is something even awful in the nearness it brings." But if Mrs. Wharton assented to that, she also—after an interval, during which they selected Browning's "By the Fireside" and his "Any Wife to Any Husband" as the best poetic examples—went on to exclaim, with a kind of desolation, "Ah, the poverty, the miserable poverty, of any love that lies outside of marriage, of any love that is not a living together, a sharing of all!"

It is because of some such principle that Halston Merrick, in "The Long Run" (a story written a few months before the exchange just quoted), sends away his mistress Paulina Trant, when the latter offers to abandon her dreary husband and run off with him. In the course of their dialogue about the risks and sacrifices that might be in store for them, Paulina had observed with sad irony that "one way of finding out whether a risk is worth taking is *not* to take it, and then to see what one becomes in the long run, and draw one's inferences." What becomes of Halston and Paulina, as they retreat into the conventional, is in its well-cushioned manner not much less dreadful than what becomes of Ethan Frome and Mattie Silver. (One notes in passing that more often than not Edith Wharton's destroyed characters survive to take the full measure of their destruction.) Halston, who once had serious inclinations to literature, turns into a joyless bachelor, the manager of his father's iron foundry. Paulina, after her husband's death, marries "a large glossy man with...a red face," and is seen regularly at dinner parties, listening to the banal conversations with "a small unvarying smile which might have been pinned on with her ornaments," ready at the proper moment to respond with the proper sentiment. This superb and gruesome story adds to the impression that, for Edith Wharton, if the individual is offered any real choice in life, it is usually a choice between modes of defeat.

Of course, the human condition envisaged is not always so bleak in Edith Wharton's short stories, nor the alternatives so desperate; she was not so driven by a theory of life that she remained blind to variety both in experience and in narrative. In "The Letters," when Lizzie Deering discovers that her husband had not even opened the tender letters she had written him years before during the time of their courtship, she does not yield to her first impulse—to take their child and to leave him. She is stricken by the deception and by all that it implies, but she slowly adjusts "to the new image of her husband as he was." He was not, she realizes, "the hero of her dreams, but he was the man she loved, and who had loved her." The situation she now takes in and accepts—in a "last wide flash of pity and initiation"—is that "out of mean mixed substances" there had, after all, been "fashioned a love that will bear the stress of life." And in an altogether different mood, there is "The Mission of Jane," wherein Mrs. Lethbury (a woman "like a dried sponge put in water; she expanded, but she did not change her shape") and her elegant, helplessly embarrassed husband adopt a baby girl. This unspeakable child, as she grows up, assumes as her mission the relentless reform of the entire household. She fulfills that mission at last, and after hair-raising hesitation, by marrying and departing—thus allowing her parents to come together on the common ground of enormous relief, joining in fact and spirit as they had never done in two decades of marriage.

One of the seeming options for the domestically harried and entrapped, under the circumstances of modern American life, was, needless to say, the act of divorce; and it is not surprising that Mrs. Wharton (whose decree was granted in 1913) dealt with this alternative a number of times. For some years before Mrs. Wharton began writing, divorce had been "an enormous fact...in American life," as William Dean Howells had remarked when he was writing *A Modern Instance* (1882), a novel of which "the question of divorce" was to be "the moving principle." Howells complained that "it has never been treated seriously"; but following his lead, Edith Wharton did so in some of her most successful stories—among them, "The Reckoning," "The Last Asset," "Autres Temps..." and "The Other Two." She caught at the subject during the period when divorce was changing from the scandalous to the acceptable and even the commonplace; and it is just the shifting, uncertain *status* of the act on which Mrs. Wharton so knowingly concentrated. In her treatment, it was not so much the grounds for divorce that interested her (though she could be both amusing and bitter on this score), and much less the technicalities involved. It was the process by which an individual might be forced to confront the fact itself—especially in its psychological and social consequences—as something irreversible and yet sometimes wickedly paradoxical. (The contemporary reader, for whom, again, divorce may seem little more than tangential to the main business of the personal life, can enjoy a shock of recognition in reading the stories cited.) Divorce, thus considered, was also the source of a revelation: about manners and the stubborn attitudes they may equally express or conceal; about the essential nature of the sexual relation; about the lingering injuries to the psyche that divorce, given certain social pressures and prejudices, may inflict on all concerned.

It is all those things that Julia Westall is driven to understand in "The Reckoning." Julia had been a young woman with "her own views on the immorality of marriage"; she had been a leading practitioner, in New York Bohemia, of "the new dispensation... *Thou shalt not be unfaithful—to thyself.*" She had only acted on her own foolishly selfish ideas when she brusquely demanded release from her first husband; now she is reduced to hysteria and almost to madness when her second husband, who had been her disciple in these matters, makes the same demand of her. "The Reckoning" is somewhat overwritten, and it is uneven in tone; it is an anecdote, really, about the biter bit, though by no means unmoving. A richer and more convincingly terrible story is "Autres Temps...," the account of Mrs. Lidcote's forced return from a dream of freedom to "the grim edges of reality," a reality here constituted by the social mores, at once cheerfully relaxing and cruelly fixed, about divorce. Years before (the story was written in 1916), Mrs. Lidcote had suffered disgrace and exile because she had been divorced and remarried. Now it appears that times must have changed, for her daughter has done the very same thing without arousing the faintest social disapproval. Mrs. Lidcote dares to return to America; but after two experiences of profoundest humiliation, she learns that for her the times and the mores will never change. Few moments in Edith Wharton's short stories are as telling in their exquisite agony as those in which first Mrs. Lidcote's daughter and then her kindly would-be lover acknowledge by a slow, irrepressible and all-devouring blush the truth of *her* situation. Those moments have the more expansiveness of meaning, because few of Edith Wharton's heroines accept the grim reality with greater courage or compassion for their destroyers. And in few stories are the radical ironies of social change more powerfully handled.

"The Other Two" is a yet more brilliant dissection of the mannered life, and it is very likely the best story Mrs. Wharton ever wrote. It can stand as the measure of her achievement in the short story form; for it has scarcely any plot—it has no real arrangement of incidents, there being too few incidents to arrange—but consists almost entirely in the leisurely, coolly comic process by which a situation is revealed to those involved it it. It is revealed in particular to Waythorn, his wife's third husband, who discovers himself in mysterious but indissoluble league with "the other two," as exceedingly different in background or in style as all three are from one another. Waythorn comes by degrees to perceive that the wife he adores, and who had seemed to him so vivid and above all so unique a personality, is in fact (and in a disconcertingly appropriate figure) "'as easy as an old shoe'—a shoe that too many feet had worn. ... Alice Haskett—Alice Varick—Alice Waythorn—she had been each in turn, and had left hanging to each name a little of her privacy, a little of her personality, a little of the inmost self where the unknown god abides."

Those last echoing phrases add up to a splendid formulation, and they contain a good deal of Edith Wharton's basic psychology. But for the most part, the rhetoric of "The Other Two" does not need or attempt to rise to such overt and summary statement. Everything is communicated, rather, by the exact notation of manners—of dress and gesture and expression: of Haskett's "made-up tie attached with an elastic," and Waythorn's uneasy distaste for it; of Varick sitting by Mrs. Waythorn at a ball and failing to rise when Waythorn strolls by; of Mrs. Waythorn absent-mindedly giving her husband cognac with his coffee. The story's last sentence brings an exemplary little comedy of man-

ners (which could serve as a model in any effort to define the
genre) to a perfect conclusion. The three husbands are together
for the first time, in the Waythorn drawing room. Mrs. Waythorn
enters and suggests brightly, easily, that everyone must want a
cup of tea.

> The two visitors, as if drawn by her smile, advanced to receive the
> cups she held out.
>   She glanced about for Waythorn, and he took the third cup with
> a laugh.

III

Edith Wharton declared her affection for the supernatural tale
in both *The Writing of Fiction* and the preface to *Ghosts;* and
though, like the historical romances, her ghost stories are a pro-
vocatively mixed lot, she displayed her skill in this category often
enough to be ranked among its modern masters. For an addict
like the present commentator, "Kerfol," "Mr. Jones," "Pomegranate Seed," and "All Souls'" are thoroughly beguiling and
rereadable; while "The Eyes" verges on the extraordinary and
contains something of "the appalling moral significance" Mrs.
Wharton discerned in "The Turn of the Screw," that novella of
Henry James for which she had a sort of absolute admiration.
Most of these stories deal, as I have said, with the marriage
question, but they deal with it in an atmosphere which is a curious
and artful blend of the passionate and violent with the muted and
remote. In "Kerfol," an American visitor to Brittany encounters
what turn out to be the ghosts of a pack of dogs, spectral survivors of a seventeenth century domestic drama of sadism, revenge and madness. In "Mr. Jones," the ghost of a majordomo
who a century earlier had served as jailer to an unfortunate lady,
the deaf-and-dumb wife of his villainous master, endures to commit a contemporary murder. In "Pomegranate Seed," Kenneth
Ashby, widowed and remarried, vanishes after receiving a series
of letters written in a hand so faint as to be almost illegible; his
second wife is left with the belated and blood-chilling knowledge
of their source. The genre of the supernatural, Mrs. Wharton
conjectures in "Telling a Short Story," did not derive from
French or Russian writing, but "seems to have come from mys-

terious Germanic and Armorican" (i.e. Breton) "forests, from lands of long twilight and wailing winds." She might have added that it seems to derive also from recesses of the imagination other and perhaps deeper than those which give rise to realistic fiction. But this may be one part of what she had in mind when, in the preface to *Ghosts,* she contended that "the teller" of ghost stories "should be well frightened in the telling."

With the ghostly tales of Mrs. Wharton, in any event, one is inevitably interested not only in what happens in the plot, but in what happens in the telling of it. "Pomegranate Seed" offers one kind of clue. In the preface to *Ghosts,* while lamenting a decline in the practice and enjoyment of ghost stories, Mrs. Wharton speaks of the many inquiries she had received about the title of "Pomegranate Seed," and refers a bit cryptically to the deplorable contemporary ignorance of "classical fairy lore." The reference is no doubt to the legend of Persephone (in the Latin version), who was abducted by Pluto, god of the underworld, and who would have been entirely liberated by Jupiter if she had not broken her vow to Pluto—of total abstinence from food—by eating some pomegranate seeds; whereafter she was required to spend the dark winter months of each year in the underworld, returning to earth only with the arrival of spring.

The connection with Mrs. Wharton's tale is superficially slender, especially since the Persephone story is usually interpreted as a seasonal myth—the annual return of winter darkness and sterility, the annual rebirth of nature in the spring. But theorists of a Freudian or, alternately, a Jungian persuasion, have made out a strong sexual motif in most ancient mythology, and find the sources of myth as much in sexual struggles and yearnings as in the cycle of nature. The story of Persephone yields quickly to such an interpretation, and so obviously does "Pomegranate Seed." Edith Wharton, in this view, has taken a familiar story of sexual combat—two women battling over one man, and the man himself divided between conflicting erotic leanings—and turned it into a ghost story: which is then cast into a dimly mythic pattern, and carefully labeled for our guidance. It is thus the dead wife Elsie who has assumed the role of Pluto and has summoned her spouse to leave his earthly existence and cohabit with her in the land of the dead—Ashby having broken *his* vow of constancy by remarrying.

In this and other tales, in short, Mrs. Wharton's imagination was moving in the direction of the mythic, but arriving only at the way station of the ghostly and fantastic. This, for Mrs. Wharton, was far enough; for she was doing no more than adopting the Victorian habit (itself a gesture toward the mythic) of "distancing" the most intense and private sexual feelings by projecting them in the various forms of fantasy. It is notable, for example, that the ghostly context permits a more direct acknowledgment of sexual experience than we normally find in the dramas of manners and the social life. In "The Lady's Maid's Bell," the action turns on the brutish physical demands made by one Brympton upon his fastidious wife: "I turned sick," says the narrator, the English-born maid Hartley, "to think what some ladies have to endure and hold their tongues about." Nor is there much mystery about the nature of Farmer Rutledge's bewitchment by the ghost of Ora Brand in "Bewitched," an artificial yarn which strives for effect by converting the figurative into the literal. But the expertly harrowing "All Souls'" indicates how erotic material could be transmuted into the terrifying without losing either its essential nature or its power.

On the last day of October, Sara Clayburn encounters a strange woman who has come to see one of the maidservants on the large staff of her Connecticut home. Later, Mrs. Clayburn sprains her ankle and is forced to her bed. The maidservant fails to appear next morning, and Mrs. Clayburn hobbles through the house in great pain, searching for help. The house is empty, the electricity cut off, the fire dead. She spends a day and night in panic-stricken solitude. When she awakens again, the servants are at their appointed tasks, all of them insisting that there had been no such passage of time, and the entire episode simply a bad dream. Exactly a year later, Mrs. Clayburn sees the same strange woman approaching the house, and she flees in hysterics to her cousin in New York. Together, they speculate that the woman must have been a "ketch," who had come to escort the maid and the other servants to a nearby "coven." The story is a fine and highly original narrative study of steadily increasing fear; and I am sure that what one remembers is Mrs. Clayburn's painful progress through the empty house. But the full force of "All Souls'" comes from the retrospective juxtaposition of Mrs. Clayburn's experience and the gathering which is the cause of it. Edith Wharton knew well enough that a coven was an exercise in witchcraft which usually led to the wildest erotic activities. And to put it in a ruinously oversimplified manner, Mrs. Clayburn's terrors—her sense of physically trapped solitude, the loss of her grip on reality, her later hysteria—are in fact her intuitive moral and psychological *reaction* to the coven.

To what extent, in the stories under discussion, was Edith Wharton's imagination working with her own private passions, impulses and fears? To what extent was she "distancing" elements in her personal life by converting them into the eerie or setting them in a far-gone age, or both (as in "Kerfol")? To a very considerable extent, I should suppose. It is easy enough—so easy that I did not pause to say so—to find reflections of Mrs. Wharton's experience of marriage with Teddy Wharton in the stories examined earlier: for example, in "The Letters"; to which we could add "The Lamp of Psyche," in which Delia Corbett's attitude to her husband, after she has detected his basic flaw, changes from "passionate worship" to "tolerant affection"; and the first of the little fables in "The Valley of Childish Things," where the female figure matures after going out into the great world (i.e., Europe) and coming back home, but the male on his return simply reverts to the childish. With the ghostly tales, and with those of the historical romance which can be helpfully included here, the problem is usually more complex, and exactly because the elements being converted were so much more deeply rooted, so much a matter of obscure or wayward or almost inexpressible emotions—and perhaps so alien to Edith Wharton's temperament, as the latter has normally been understood. But even in "Kerfol" (to take an apparently extreme instance), one can, by making a number of substitutions, come upon a fantasy of savage personal revenge, a violent but purely imagined repayment for a series of psychological cruelties.

There the translation from life into story is complete; "Kerfol" needs no biographical interpretation to give it interest. Sometimes, however, Mrs. Wharton's imagination was overcome by her personal feeling, and she failed to make the full translation: which explains, I believe, the unevenness mentioned at the start of this section. "The Hermit and the Wild Woman"—which can stand for several of the romances (including "The Duchess at

Prayer" and "Dieu d'Amour")—is instructive, for it is just such a failure; *its* interest is almost entirely biographical. This story, which takes place in late medieval Italy, is told in a somewhat pretentious style founded on that of the lives of the saints. A so-called Wild Woman has escaped from a convent because she was forbidden to bathe herself; she wanders the mountains till she meets with a Hermit of singular austerity; she performs many miraculous cures, but she is constantly chided by the holy man for her continuing desire to clean and refresh her body in the mountain lake; finally she drowns in the water, and the Hermit realizes too late that her nature was yet more saintly and devout than his own. It is a tedious and contrived piece of work; and one is at a loss to understand why Mrs. Wharton wrote it—until it dawns on one that this is Mrs. Wharton's effort to make a story out of a deeply troubled period in her life, while retaining her privacy by placing the experience in the far temporal distance and the most remote possible atmosphere. It becomes uncomfortably clear that the relation between the Wild Woman and the Hermit is an elementary version, at several kinds of remove, of the relation between Edith Wharton and Walter Berry, during the period when she was escaping or trying to escape from her own convent, her marriage.

The story was written in 1906, and it is fundamentally an account of what was transpiring between the two at that very time. Something of this was made public a few years ago by Wayne Andrews in his introduction to *The Best Short Stories of Edith Wharton,* where he quoted several passages from Mrs. Wharton's "diary" for 1907. It seems in fact not to have been a diary, properly speaking, but a fragment of autobiographical narrative written in diary form. In it, Mrs. Wharton recorded her burning desire (she speaks of a "flame" of feeling) for total intimacy with Walter Berry, along with her tormented meditations on the sinfulness or lack of it of the extramarital physical relation. She indicated her own belief in, as it were, the holiness of the sensuous life: "I feel that all the mysticism in me—and the transcendentalism that in other women turns to religion—were poured into my feeling for you."

So her Wild Woman's exalted spirituality found paradoxical but persuasive expression in her ineradicable need to "sleep under the free heaven and wash the dust from my body in cool water." But Berry, like the Hermit, evidently recoiled in some dismay at these revealed longings though Mrs. Wharton, discreet even in privacy, only hinted at his tendency to smash their most precious moments together. "It was as if there stood between us... the frailest of glass cups, filled with a rare and colorless wine— and with a gesture you broke the glass and spilled the drops." The end of "The Hermit and the Wild Woman" thus appears as an only too familiar act of self-consoling prophecy: too late, her sometime lover would appreciate the true value of what he had missed.[1]

"The Eyes," written in 1910, springs from the same cluster of longings and resentments, but it is an immeasurably superior story; the author's personal feelings have here been perfectly translated into a nearly seamless work of art. Andrew Culwin's reminiscence of his two acts of seemingly spontaneous generosity —the proposal of marriage to his cousin Alice Nowell, his pretence of admiration for the literary talent of young Noyes—and of the two ugly red sneering eyes which appeared after both incidents to glare at him derisively through the night: this is all of a piece. Gilbert Noyes, the godlike youth who turns up suddenly in Rome, is also a cousin of Alice Nowell's, and Culwin's fear of wounding him by making plain his literary ineptness is confused by some vague sense of remorse over abandoning Alice three years before. But the turn of the screw in *this* story is the fact that Frenham, one of the two men listening to Culwin's hideous and shockingly unconscious self-disclosure, is another attractive young neophyte, Noyes's most recent successor. He is the latest proof of the "ogreish metaphor" of one of Culwin's friends, that the old man "liked 'em juicy." To the climax of Cul-

---

[1]This reading is confirmed in part by a narrative poem called "Ogrin the Hermit," which Mrs. Wharton wrote in the spring of 1909. The story, briefly, is this: Tristan and Iseult, fleeing Iseult's husband, King Mark, take refuge with the Hermit Ogrin. In the days that follow, while Tristan is away hunting, the Hermit pleads with Iseult to give up her sinful life with Tristan; but Iseult replies with an eloquent defense of the innocence, again almost the holiness, of pure and dedicated erotic love. The Hermit, despite himself, is convinced of the rightness of her course. The poem is rather better, as a literary exercise, than "The Hermit and the Wild Woman," and it is of still greater biographical interest, since a third figure (clearly not the husband) has been added.

win's reminiscence, there is added the climax of the tale itself, when Frenham sits transfixed with horror. In the face of his mentor, the very shaper of his own life and personality, Frenham has seen what Culwin remembered seeing: eyes that reminded him "of vampires with a taste for young flesh."

It is not only that the eyes represent Culwin's real self, the egotistical and gradually evil self that (like that of Lavington in "The Triumph of Night") lies hidden behind his "cold and drafty" intelligence, his utter detachment, his occasional moral contentment. It is also that, on the two occasions of generosity, his good conscience—his "glow of self-righteousness"—is the glare of the eyes. For a character like Culwin's, the generous gesture is a necessary concession to the ego; it is a feeding of the ego on the tenderness of flesh and spirit; and a part of him knows it. Like Henry James, Edith Wharton was alert to the sinister impulses that can sometimes take the form of moral self-satisfaction. But the implications of this astonishing story go beyond that, and open up almost endlessly to thoughtful scrutiny.

Culwin's treatment of Alice Nowell is more than paralleled by his treatment of Noyes. It is explained by it; and all the carefully chosen (and as the manuscript shows, painstakingly revised) details about the old man, about his habits and tastes, his manner of speech and way of life, combine to give a chilling portrait of a dilettantish, devouringly selfish homosexual. The two victims coalesce; indeed, Miss Nowell's Christian name was originally Grace, before Mrs. Wharton (as it appears) decided that it would be too schematic to provide both victims with the same initials. Nevertheless, when we put together the young woman with her unreproachful grief (still unreproachful, one surmises, after Culwin had fled from her) and the aspiring young writer of fiction, we begin to identify a single and very real personality, and to identify "The Eyes" as the projection by Mrs. Wharton of her most buried feelings about Walter Berry. It is, as Louis Auchincloss has pointed out, the Walter Berry as seen in the resentful perspective of Percy Lubbock: "a dogmatic, snobbish egotist and the evil genius of Edith Wharton's life." But the perspective on this occasion at least was also Mrs. Wharton's—though her imagination was in such firm control of her materials that it is unlikely she ever quite knew what she had accomplished. Yet surely, as this beautifully composed story took shape, Mrs. Wharton must have been, however obscurely, more than a little frightened in the telling.[2]

[2]Ironically but tellingly, Berry liked the story, and Mrs. Wharton was pleased that he did. "The ghost story...*is* good," she wrote a friend; "even Walter says so!"

Reflections on Willa Cather

by Katherine Anne Porter

I never knew her at all, nor anyone who did know her; do not to this day. When I was a young writer in New York I knew she was there, and sometimes wished that by some charming chance I might meet up with her; but I never did, and it did not occur to me to seek her out. I had never felt that my condition of beginning authorship gave me a natural claim on the attention of writers I admired, such as Henry James and W. B. Yeats. Some proper instinct told me that all of any importance they had to say to me was in their printed pages, mine to use as I could. Still it would have been nice to have seen them, just to remember how they looked. There are three or four great ones, gone now, that I feel, too late, I should not have missed. Willa Cather was one of them.

There exist large numbers of critical estimates of her work, appreciations; perhaps even a memoir or two, giving glimpses of her personal history—I have never read one. She was not, in the popular crutch-word to describe almost any kind of sensation, "exciting"; so far as I know, nobody, not even one of the Freudian school of critics, ever sat up nights with a textbook in one hand and her works in the other, reading between the lines to discover how much sexual autobiography could be mined out of her stories. I remember only one photograph—Steichen's—made in middle life, showing a big plain smiling woman, her arms crossed easily over a girl-scout sort of white blouse, with a ragged part in her hair. She seemed, as the French say, "well seated" and not very outgoing. Even the earnestly amiable, finely shaped eyes, the left one faintly askew, were in some mysterious way not expressive, lacking as they did altogether that look of strangeness which a strange vision is supposed to give to the eye of any real artist, and very often does. One doesn't have to be a genius absolutely to get this look, it is often quite enough merely to believe one is a genius; and to have had the wild vision only once is enough — the afterlight stays, even if, in such case, it is phosphorescence instead of living fire.

Well, Miss Cather looks awfully like somebody's big sister, or maiden aunt, both of which she was. No genius ever looked less like one, according to the romantic popular view, unless it was her idol, Flaubert, whose photographs could pass easily for those of any paunchy country squire indifferent to his appearance. Like him, none of her genius was in her looks, only in her works. Flaubert was a good son, adoring uncle of a niece, devoted to his friends, contemptuous of the mediocre, obstinate in his preferences, fiercely jealous of his privacy, unyielding to the death in his literary principles and not in the slightest concerned with what was fashionable. No wonder she loved him. She had been rebuffed a little at first, not by his astronomical standards in art — none could be too high for her — but by a certain coldness of heart in him. She soon got over that; it became for her only another facet of his nobility of mind.

Very early she had learned to reverence that indispensable faculty of aspiration of the human mind toward perfection called, in morals and the arts, nobility. She was born to the idea and brought up in it: first in a little crowded farmhouse in Virginia, and later, the eldest of seven children, in a little crowded ranch house in Nebraska. She had, as many American country people did have in those times and places, literate parents and grandparents, soundly educated and deeply read, educated, if not always at schools, always at their own firesides. Two such, her grandmothers, taught her from her infancy. Her sister, Mrs. Auld, in Palo Alto, California, told it like this:

"She mothered us all, took care of us, and there was a lot to do in such a big family. She learned Greek and Latin from our grandmothers before she ever got to go to school. She used to go, after we lived in Red Cloud, to read Latin and Greek with a little old man who kept a general store down the road. In the evenings for entertainment—there was nowhere to go, you know, almost nothing to see or hear—she entertained us, it was good as a theater for us! She told us long stories, some she made up herself, and some were her versions of legends and fairy tales she had read; she taught us Greek mythology this way, Homer; and tales from the Old Testament. We were all story tellers," said her sister, "all of us wanted to be the one to tell the stories, but she was the one who told them. And we loved to listen all of us to her, when maybe we would not have listened to each other."

She was not the first nor the last American writer to be formed in this system of home education; at one time it was the customary education for daughters, many of them never got to school at all or expected to; but they were capable of educating their grandchildren, as this little history shows. To her last day Willa Cather was the true child of her plain-living, provincial farming people, with their aristocratic ways of feeling and thinking; poor, but not poverty-stricken for a moment; rock-based in character, a character shaped in an old school of good manners, good morals, and the unchallenged assumption that classic culture was their birthright; the belief that knowledge of great art and great thought was a good in itself not to be missed for anything; she subscribed to it all with her whole heart, and in herself there was the vein of iron she had inherited from a long line of people who had helped to break wildernesses and to found a new nation in such faiths. When you think of the whole unbelievable history, how did anything like this survive? Yet it did, and this life is one of the proofs.

I have not much interest in anyone's personal history after the tenth year, not even my own. Whatever one was going to be was all prepared for before that. The rest is merely confirmation, extension, development. Childhood is the fiery furnace in which we are melted down to essentials and that essential shaped for good. While I have been reading again Willa Cather's essays and occasional papers, and thinking about her, I remembered a sentence from the diaries of Anne Frank, who died in the concentration camp in Bergen-Belsen just before she was sixteen years old. At less than fifteen, she wrote: "I have had a lot of sorrow, but who hasn't, at my age?"

In Miss Cather's superb little essay on Katherine Mansfield, she speaks of childhood and family life: "I doubt whether any contemporary writer has made one feel more keenly the many kinds of personal relations which exist in an everyday 'happy family' who are merely going on with their daily lives, with no crises or shocks or bewildering complications.... Yet every individual in that household (even the children) is clinging passionately to his individual soul, is in terror of losing it in the family flavor...the mere struggle to have anything of one's own, to be oneself at all, creates an element of strain which keeps everybody almost at breaking point.

"...Even in harmonious families there is this double life... the one we can observe in our neighbor's household, and, underneath, another—secret and passionate and intense—which is the real life that stamps the faces and gives character to the voices of our friends. Always in his mind each member is escaping, running away, trying to break the net which circumstances and his own affections have woven about him. One realizes that human relationships are the tragic necessity of human life; that they can never be wholly satisfactory, that every ego is half the time greedily seeking them, and half the time pulling away from them."

This is masterly and water-clear and autobiography enough for me: my mind goes with tenderness to the big lonely slow-moving girl who happened to be an artist coming back from reading Latin and Greek with the old storekeeper, helping with the housework, then sitting by the fireplace to talk down an assertive brood of brothers and sisters, practicing her art on them, refusing to be lost among them—the longest-winged one who would fly free at last.

I am not much given to reading about authors, or not until I have read what they have to say for themselves. I found Willa Cather's books for myself, early, and felt no need for intermediaries between me and them. My reading went on for a good many years, one by one as they appeared: *O Pioneers!; The Song of the Lark; My Ántonia; Youth and the Bright Medusa; Death Comes for the Archbishop; Obscure Destinies;* just these, and no others, I do not know why, and never anything since, until I read her notebooks about two years ago. Those early readings began in Texas, just before World War I, before ever I left home; they ended in Paris, twenty years later, after the longest kind of journey.

With her first book I was reading also Henry James, W. B.

Yeats, Joseph Conrad, my introduction to "modern" literature, for I was brought up on solid reading, too, well aged. About the same time I read Gertrude Stein's *Tender Buttons,* for sale at a little bookshop with a shoeshine stand outside; inside you could find magazines, books, newspapers in half-a-dozen languages, *avant-garde* and radical and experimental; this in a Texas coast town of less than ten thousand population but very polyglot and full of world travelers. I could make little headway with Miss Stein beyond the title. It was plain that she meant "tender buds" and I wondered why she did not say so. It was the beginning of my quarrel with a certain school of "modern" writing in which poverty of feeling and idea were disguised, but not well enough, in tricky techniques and disordered syntax. A year or two after *Tender Buttons* I was reading Joyce's *Dubliners,* and maybe only a young beginning writer of that time, with some preparation of mind by the great literature of the past, could know what a revelation that small collection of matchless stories could be. It was not a shock, but a revelation, a further unfolding of the deep world of the imagination. I had never heard of Joyce. By the pure chance of my roving curiosity, I picked up a copy of the book at that little shoeshine bookstore. It was a great day.

By the time I reached Paris, I had done my long apprenticeship, published a small book of my own, and had gone like a house afire through everything "new"—that word meant something peculiar to the times—absolutely everything "new" that was being published; also in music; also painting. I considered almost any painting with the varnish still wet, the artist standing by, so to speak, as more interesting than anything done even the year before. But some of the painters were Klee, Juan Gris, Modigliani. ... I couldn't listen to music happily if it wasn't hot from the composer's brain, preferably conducted or played by himself. Still, some of the music was Stravinsky's. I was converted to the harpsichord by the first New York recital of Wanda Landowska. In the theater I preferred dress rehearsals, or even just rehearsals, to the finished performance; I was mad about the ballet and took lessons off and on with a Russian for two years; I even wrote a ballet libretto way back in 1920 for a young Mexican painter and scene designer who gave the whole thing to Pavlova, who danced it in many countries but not in New York, because the scenery was done on paper, was inflammable and she was not allowed to use it in New York. I saw photographs, however, and I must say they did not look in the least like anything I had provided for in the libretto. It was most unsatisfactory.

What has this to do with Willa Cather? A great deal. I had had time to grow up, to consider, to look again, to begin finding my way a little through the inordinate clutter and noise of my immediate day, in which very literally everything in the world was being pulled apart, torn up, turned wrong side out and upside down; almost no frontiers left unattacked, governments and currencies falling; even the very sexes seemed to be changing back and forth and multiplying weird, unclassifiable genders. And every day, in the arts, as in schemes of government and organized crime, there was, there had to be, something New.

Alas, or thank God, depending on the way you feel about it, there comes that day when today's New begins to look a little like yesterday's New, and then more and more so; you begin to suffer slightly from a sense of sameness or repetition: that painting, that statue, that music, that kind of writing, that way of thinking and feeling, that revolution, that political doctrine—is it really New? The answer is simply no, and if you are really in a perverse belligerent mood, you may add a half-truth—no, and it never was. Looking around at the debris, you ask has newness merely for its own sake any virtue? And you find that all along you had held and wound in your hand through the maze an unbreakable cord on which one by one, hardly knowing it, you had strung your life's treasures; it was as if they had come of themselves, while you were seeking and choosing and picking up and tossing away again, down all sorts of bypaths and up strange stairs and into queer corners; and there they were, things old and new, the things you loved first and those you loved last, all together and yours, and no longer old or new, but outside of time and beyond the reach of change, even your own; for that part of your life they belong to was in some sense made by them; if they went, all that part of your life would be mutilated, unrecognizable. While you hold and wind that cord with its slowly accumulating, weightless, unaccountable riches, the maze seems a straight road; you look back through all the fury you have come through, when it seemed so much, and so dismayingly, destruction, and so much just the pervasively trivial, stupid, or malignant-dwarfish tricks: fur-lined cups as sculpture, symphonies written for kitchen batteries, experiments on language very similar to the later Nazi surgical experiments of cutting and uniting human nerve ends never meant to touch each other: so many perversities crowding in so close you could hardly see beyond them. Yet look, you shared it, you were part of it, you even added to the confusion, so busy being new yourself. The fury and waste and clamor was, after all, just what you had thought it was in the first place, even if you had lost sight of it later—life, in a word, and great glory came of it, and splendid things that will go on living cleared of all the rubbish thrown up around their creation. Things you would have once thought incompatible to eternity take their right places in peace, in proper scale and order, in your mind—in your blood. They become that marrow in your bones where the blood is renewed.

I had liked best of all Willa Cather's two collections of short stories. They live still with morning freshness in my memory, their clearness, warmth of feeling, calmness of intelligence, an ample human view of things; in short the sense of an artist at work in whom one could have complete confidence: not even the prose attracted my attention from what the writer was saying—really saying, and not just in the words. Also I remember well my deeper impression of reserve—a reserve that was personal because it was a matter of temperament, the grain of the mind; yet conscious too, and practiced deliberately: almost a method, a technique, but not assumed. It was instead a manifesting, proceeding from the moral nature of the artist, morality extended to aesthetics—not aesthetics as morality but simply a development of both faculties along with all the others until the whole being was indivisibly one, the imagination and its expression fused and fixed.

A magnificent state, no doubt, at which to arrive; but it should be the final one, and Miss Cather seemed to be there almost from the first. What was it? For I began to have an image of her as a kind of lighthouse, or even a promontory, some changeless phenomenon of art or nature or both. I have a peculiar antipathy to thinking of anyone I know in symbols or mythical characters and this finally quietly alienated me from her, from her very fine books, from any feeling that she was a living, working artist in our time. It is hard to explain, for it was a question of tone, of implication, and what else? Finally, after a great while, I decided that Miss Cather's reserve amounted to a deliberate withholding of some vital part of herself as artist; not as if she had hidden herself at the center of her mystery but was still there to be disclosed at last; no, she had absented herself willfully.

I was quite wrong of course. She is exactly at the center of her own mystery, where she belongs. My immoderate reading of our two or three invaluably afflicted giants of contemporary literature, and their abject army of camp followers and imitators, had blurred temporarily my perception of that thin line separating self-revealment from self-exhibition. Miss Cather had never any intention of using fiction or any other form of writing as a device for showing herself off. She was not Paul in travesty, nor the opera singer in "The Diamond Mine," nor that girl with the clear eyes who became an actress: above all, not the Lost Lady. Of course she was all of them. How not? She made all of them out of herself, where else could they have taken on life?

Her natural lack of picturesqueness was also a good protective coloring: it saved her from the invasive prying of hangers-on: and no "school" formed in her name. The young writers did not swarm over her with flattery, manuscripts in hand, meaning to use her for all she was worth; publishers did not waylay her with seductions the instant her first little book appeared; all S. S. McClure could think of to do for her, after he published *The Troll Garden,* was to offer her a job as one of his editors on *McClure's Magazine,* where she worked hard for six mortal years before it seems to have occurred to her that she was not being a writer, after all, which was what she had started out for. So she quit her job, and the next year, more or less, published *Alexander's Bridge,* of which she afterward repented, for reasons that were to last her a lifetime. The scene, London, was strange and delightful to her; she was trying to make a novel out of some interesting people in what seemed to her exotic situations, instead of out of something she really knew about with more than the top of her mind. "London is supposed to be more engaging than, let us say, Gopher Prairie," she remarks, "even if the writer knows Gopher Prairie very well and London very casually."

She realized at once that *Alexander's Bridge* was a mistake, her wrong turning, which could not be retraced too instantly and entirely. It was a very pretty success, and could have been her finish, except that she happened to be Willa Cather. For years she still found people who liked that book, but they couldn't fool her. She knew what she had done. So she left New York and went to Arizona for six months, not for repentance but for refreshment, and found there a source that was to refresh her for years to come. Let her tell of her private apocalypse in her own words: "I did no writing down there, but I recovered from the conventional editorial point of view."

She then began to write a book for herself— *O Pioneers!*—and it was "a different process altogether. Here there was no arranging or 'inventing'; everything was spontaneous and took its own place, right or wrong. This was like taking a ride through a familiar country on a horse that knew the way, on a fine morning when you felt like riding. The other was like riding in a park, with someone not altogether congenial, to whom you had to be talking all the time."

What are we to think? For certainly here is a genius who simply will not cater to our tastes for drama, who refuses to play the role in any way we have been accustomed to seeing it played. She wrote with immense sympathy about Stephen Crane: "There is every evidence that he was a reticent and unhelpful man, with no warmhearted love of giving out opinions." If she had said "personal confidences" she could as well have been writing about herself. But she was really writing about Stephen Crane and stuck to her subject. Herself, she gave out quite a lot of opinions, not all of them warmhearted, in the course of two short little books, the second a partial reprint of the first. You hardly realize how many and how firm and how cogent while reading her fine pure direct prose, hearing through it a level, well-tempered voice saying very good, sensible right things with complete authority—things not in fashion but close to here and now and always, not like a teacher or a mother—like an artist—until, after you have closed the book, her point of view begins to accumulate and take shape in your mind.

Freud had happened: but Miss Cather continued to cite the old Hebrew prophets, the Greek dramatists, Goethe, Shakespeare, Dante, Tolstoy, Flaubert, and such for the deeper truths of human nature, both good and evil. She loved Shelley, Wordsworth, Walter Pater, without any reference to their public standing at the time. In her essay, "The Novel Démeublé," she had the inspired notion to bring together for purposes of comparison Balzac and Prosper Merimée; she preferred Merimée on the ground quite simply that he was the better artist: you have to sort out Balzac's meanings from a great dusty warehouse of irrelevant vain matter — furniture, in a word. Once got at, they are as vital as ever. But Merimée is as vital, and you cannot cut one sentence without loss from his stories. The perfect answer to the gross power of the one, the too-finished delicacy of the other was, of course, Flaubert.

Stravinsky had happened; but she went on being dead in love with Wagner, Beethoven, Schubert, Gluck, especially *Orpheus,* and almost any opera. She was music-mad, and even Ravel's *La Valse* enchanted her; perhaps also even certain later music, but she has not mentioned it in these papers.

The Nude had Descended the Staricase with an epoch-shaking tread but she remained faithful to Puvis de Chavannes, whose wall paintings in the Panthéon of the legend of St. Genevieve inspired the form and tone of *Death Comes for the Archbishop.* She longed to tell old stories as simply as that, as deeply centered in the core of experience without extraneous detail as in the lives of the saints in *The Golden Legend.* She loved Courbet, Rembrandt, Millet and the sixteenth-century Dutch and Flemish painters, with their "warmly furnished interiors" but always with a square window open to the wide gray sea, where the masts of the great Dutch fleets were setting out to "ply quietly on all the waters of the globe. ..."

Joyce had happened: or perhaps we should say, *Ulysses,* for the work has now fairly absorbed the man we knew. I believe that this is true of all artists of the first order. They are not magnified in their work, they disappear in it, consumed by it. That subterranean upheaval of language caused not even the barest tremor in Miss Cather's firm, lucid sentences. There is good internal evidence that she read a great deal of contemporary literature, contemporary over a stretch of fifty years, and think what contemporaries they were—from Tolstoy and Hardy and James and Chekhov to Gide and Proust and Joyce and Lawrence and Virginia Woolf, to Sherwood Anderson and Theodore Dreiser: the first names that come to mind. There was a regiment of them; it was as rich and fruitfully disturbing a period as literature has to show for several centuries. And it did make an enormous change. Miss Cather held firmly to what she had found for herself, did her own work in her own way as all the others were doing each in his unique way, and did help greatly to save and reassert and illustrate the validity of certain great and dangerously threatened principles of art. Without too much fuss, too—and is quietly disappearing into her work altogether, as we might expect.

Mr. Maxwell Geismar wrote a book about her and some others, called *The Last of the Provincials*. Not having read it I do not know his argument; but he has a case: she is a provincial; and I hope not the last. She was a good artist, and all true art is provincial in the most realistic sense: of the very time and place of its making, out of human beings who are so particularly limited by their situation, whose faces and names are real and whose lives begin each one at an individual unique center. Indeed, Willa Cather was as provincial as Hawthorne or Flaubert or Turgenev, as little concerned with aesthetics and as much with morals as Tolstoy, as obstinately reserved as Melville. In fact she always reminds me of very good literary company, of the particularly admirable masters who formed her youthful tastes, her thinking and feeling.

She is a curiously immovable shape, monumental, virtue itself in her art and a symbol of virtue—like certain churches, in fact, or exemplary women, revered and neglected. Yet like these again, she has her faithful friends and true believers, even so to speak her lovers, and they last a lifetime, and after: the only kind of bond she would recognize or require or respect.

Willa Cather

by Lionel Trilling

I

In 1922 Willa Cather wrote an essay called "The Novel Démeublé" in which she pleaded for a movement to throw the "furniture" out of the novel—to get rid, that is, of all the social fact that Balzac and other realists had felt to be so necessary for the understanding of modern character. "Are the banking system and the Stock Exchange worth being written about at all?" Miss Cather asked, and she replied that they were not. Among the things which had no "proper place in imaginative art"—because they cluttered the scene and prevented the free play of the emotions—Miss Cather spoke of the factory and the whole realm of "physical sensation." Obviously, this essay was the rationale of a method which Miss Cather had partly anticipated in her early novels and which she fully developed a decade later in *Shadows on the Rock*. And it is no less obvious that this technical method is not merely a literary manner but the expression of a point of view toward which Miss Cather had always been moving—with results that, to many of her readers, can only indicate the subtle failure of her admirable talent.

If we say that Miss Cather has gone down to defeat before the actualities of American life, we put her in such interesting company that the indictment is no very terrible one. For a history of American literature must be, in Whitman's phrase, a series of "vivas for those who have failed." In our literature there are perhaps fewer completely satisfying books and certainly fewer integrated careers than there are interesting canons of work and significant life stories. Something in American life seems to pre-

"Willa Cather" by Lionel Trilling. First published in *The New Republic*, 90 (10 February 1937), pp. 10-13. Reprinted by permission of Diana Trilling.

vent the perfection of success while it produces a fascinating kind
of search or struggle, usually unavailing, which we may observe
again and again in the collected works and in the biographies of
our writers.

In this recurrent but heroic defeat, the life of the American
writer parallels the life of the American pioneer. The historian
of frontier literature, Professor Hazard, has pointed out that
Cooper's very first presentation of Deerslayer, the type of all
pioneers, shows him a nearly broken old man threatened with
jail for shooting a deer, a pitiful figure overwhelmed by the tides
of commerce and speculation. In short, to a keen observer, the
pioneer's defeat was apparent even in 1823. The subsequent
decades that opened fresh frontiers did not change the outcome
of the struggle. Ahead of the pioneer there are always the fields
of new promise, with him are the years of heart-breaking effort,
behind him are the men who profit by his toil and his hope. Miss
Cather's whole body of work is the attempt to accommodate and
assimilate her perception of the pioneer's failure. Reared on a
Nebraska farm, she saw the personal and cultural defeat at first
hand. Her forebears had marched westward to the new horizons;
her own work is a march back toward the spiritual East—toward
all that is the antithesis of the pioneer's individualism and in-
novation, toward authority and permanence, toward Rome itself.

II

The pioneer, as seen by a sophisticated intelligence like Miss
Cather's, stands in double jeopardy: he faces both the danger of
failure and the danger of success. "A pioneer...should be able
to enjoy the idea of things more than the things themselves," Miss
Cather says; disaster comes when an idea becomes an actuality.
From *O Pioneers!* to *The Professor's House,* Miss Cather's novels
portray the results of the pioneer's defeat, both in the thwarted
pettiness to which he is condemned by his material failures and in
the callous insensitivity produced by his material success. "The
world is little, people are little, human life is little," says Thea
Kronborg's derelict music teacher in *The Song of the Lark.*
"There is only one big thing—desire." When there is no longer
the opportunity for effective desire, the pioneer is doomed. But

already in Miss Cather's Nebraska youth the opportunities for effective desire had largely been removed: the frontier had been closed.

A Lost Lady, Miss Cather's most explicit treatment of the passing of the old order, is the central work of her career. Far from being the delicate minor book it is often called, it is probably her most muscular story, for it derives power from the grandeur of its theme. Miss Cather shares the American belief in the tonic moral quality of the pioneer's life; with the passing of the frontier she conceives that a great source of fortitude has been lost. Depending on a very exact manipulation of symbols, the point of *A Lost Lady* (reminiscent of Henry James's *The Sacred Fount*) is that the delicacy and charm of Marian Forrester spring not from herself, but from the moral strength of her pioneer husband. Heavy, slow, not intelligent, Forrester is one of those men who, in his own words, "dreamed the railroads across the mountains." He shares the knightly virtues which Miss Cather unquestioningly ascribes to the early settlers; "impractical to the point of magnificence," he is one of those who could "conquer but not hold." He is defeated by the men of the new money interests who "never risked anything"—and the perdition of the lost lady proceeds in the degree that she withdraws from her husband in favor of one of the sordid new men, until she finds her final degradation in the arms of an upstart vulgarian.

But though the best of the pioneer ideal is defeated by alien forces, the ideal itself, Miss Cather sees, is really an insufficient one. In her first considerable novel, *O Pioneers!,* she already wrote in an elegiac mood and with the sense that the old ideal was not enough. Alexandra Bergson, with her warm simplicity, her resourcefulness and shrewd courage, is the essence of the pioneering virtues, but she is distinguished above her neighbors because she feels that, if she is to work at all, she must believe that the world is wider than her cornfields. Her pride is not that she has triumphed over the soil, but that she has made her youngest brother, "a personality apart from the soil." The pioneer, having reached his goal at the horizons of the earth, must look to the horizons of the spirit.

The disappearance of the old frontier left Miss Cather with a heritage of the virtues in which she had been bred, but with the necessity of finding a new object for them. Looking for the new frontier, she found it in the mind. From the world of failure which she portrayed so savagely in "A Wagner Matinée" and "The Sculptor's Funeral," and from the world of fat prosperity of *One of Ours,* she could flee to the world of art; for in art one may desire illimitably. And if, conceivably, one may fail—Miss Cather's artists never do—it is still only as an artist that one may be the eternal pioneer, concerned always with "the idea of things." Thea Kronborg, of the breed of Alexandra Bergson, turns all the old energy, bogged down in mediocrity, toward music. Miss Cather rhapsodizes for her: "O eagle of eagles! Endeavor, achievement, desire, glorious striving of human art."

But art is not the only, or a sufficient, salvation from the débâcle of pioneer culture. For some vestige of the old striving after new worlds which cannot be gratified seems to spread a poison through the American soul, making it thin and unsubstantial, unable to find peace and solidity. A foreigner says to Claude Wheeler of *One of Ours,* "You Americans are always looking for something outside yourselves to warm you up, and it is no way to do. In old countries, where not very much can happen to us, we know that, and we learn to make the most of things." And with the artists, Miss Cather puts those gentle spirits who have learned to make the most of things—Neighbor Rosicky, Augusta and, preëminently, My Ántonia. Momentarily betrayed by the later developments of the frontier, Antonia at last fulfills herself in child-bearing and a busy household, expressing her "relish for life, not overdelicate but invigorating."

Indeed, "making the most of things" becomes even more important to Miss Cather than the eternal striving of art. For, she implies, in our civilization even the best ideals are bound to corruption. *The Professor's House* is the novel in which she brings the failure of the pioneer spirit into the wider field of American life. Lame as it is, it epitomizes as well as any novel of our time the disgust with life which so many sensitive Americans feel, which makes them dream of their preadolescent integration and innocent community with nature, speculate on the "release from effort" and the "eternal solitude" of death, and eventually reconcile themselves to a life "without delight." Three stories of betrayal are interwoven in this novel: the success of Professor St. Peter's history of the Spanish explorers, which tears him away from the frontier of his uncomfortable and ugly old study to set him up in an elegant but stifling new home; the sale to a foreign collector of the dead Tom Outland's Indian relics, which had made his spiritual heritage; and the commercialization of Outland's scientific discovery with its subsequent corruption of the Professor's charming family. With all of life contaminated by the rotting of admirable desires, only Augusta, the unquesting and unquestioning German Catholic seamstress, stands secure and sound.

Not the pioneering philosophy alone, but the whole poetic romanticism of the nineteenth century had been suffused with the belief that the struggle rather than the prize was admirable, that a man's reach should exceed his grasp, or what's a heaven for? Having seen the insufficiency of this philosophy Miss Cather must find another in which the goal shall be more than the search. She finds it, expectably enough, in religion. The Catholicism to which she turns is a Catholicism of culture, not of doctrine. The ideal of unremitting search, it may be said, is essentially a Protestant notion; Catholic thought tends to repudiate the ineffable and to seek the sharply defined. The quest for Moby Dick, that dangerous beast, in Protestant; the Catholic tradition selects what it can make immediate and tangible in symbol, and Miss Cather turns to the way of life that "makes the most of things," to the old settled cultures. She attaches a mystical significance to the ritual of the ordered life, to the niceties of cookery, to the supernal virtues of *things* themselves—sherry, or lettuce, or "these coppers, big and little, these brooms and clouts and brushes," which are the tools for making life itself. And with a religious ideal one may safely be a pioneer. The two priests of *Death Comes for the Archbishop* are pioneers; they happen to be successful in their enterprise, but they could not have been frustrated, Miss Cather implies, because the worth of their goal is indisputable.

From the first of her novels the Church had occupied a special and gracious place in Willa Cather's mind. She now thinks with increasing eloquence of its permanence and certainty and of "the universal human yearning for something permanent, enduring, without shadow of change." The Rock becomes her often repeated symbol: "the rock, when one comes to think of it, was the utmost expression of human need." For the Church seems to offer the possibility of satisfying that appealing definition of human happiness which Miss Cather had made as far back as *My Ántonia*— "to be dissolved in something complete and great...to become a part of something entire, whether it is sun and air, goodness and knowledge."

It is toward that dissolvement that Miss Cather is always striving. She achieves it with the "sun and air"—and perhaps few modern writers have been so successful with landscape. She can find it in goodness and in society—but only if they have the feudal constriction of the old Quebec of *Shadows on the Rock*. Nothing in modern life, no possibility, no hope, offers it to her. She conceives, as she says in the prefatory note to her volume of essays, *Not Under Forty*, that the world "broke in two in 1922 or thereabouts," and she numbers herself among the "backward," unaware that even so self-conscious and defiant a rejection of her own time must make her talent increasingly irrelevant and tangential—for any time.

III

"The early pioneer was an individualist and a seeker after the undiscovered," says F. J. Turner, "but he did not understand the richness and complexity of life as a whole." Though Miss Cather in all her work has recognized this lack of understanding of complexity and wholeness, and has attempted to transcend it, she ends, ironically enough, in a fancier but no less restricted provincialism than the one she sought to escape. For the "spirituality" of Miss Cather's latest books consists chiefly of an irritated exclusion of those elements of modern life with which she will not cope. The particular affirmation of the verities which Miss Cather makes requires that the "furniture" be thrown out, that the social and political facts be disregarded; the spiritual life cannot support the intrusion of all the facts the mind can supply. The unspeakable Joseph Joubert, the extreme type of the academic verity-seeker, says in one of his *pensées:* "'I'm hungry, I'm cold, help me!' Here is material for a good deed but not for a good work of art." Miss Cather, too, is irked by the intrusion of "physical sensations" in the novel. And one remembers Joubert's hatred of energy—he believed that it hindered the good life and scorned Balzac for his superabundant endowment of it—and one sees what is so irksome in Miss Cather's conception of ordered living: it is her implied praise of devitalization. She can recognize the energy of assiduous duty but not the energy of mind and emotion. Her order is not the channeling of insurgent human forces but their absence.

We use the word "escape" too lightly, no doubt; when we think how each generation must create its own past for the purposes of its own present, we must realize that the return to a past way of thought or of life may be the relevant criticism of the present. The only question, then, is the ends such criticism serves. Henry Adams's turn to the twelfth century was the attempt to answer the complex questions of the *Education* and to discover a better direction of energy; Eugene O'Neill's movement toward Catholic theology, crude as it may seem, has the profound interest of an energetic response to confusion. But Miss Cather's turn to the ideals of a vanished time is the weary response to weariness, to that devitalization of spirit which she so brilliantly describes in the story of Professor St. Peter. It is a weariness which comes not merely from defeat but from an exacerbated sense of personal isolation and from the narrowing of all life to the individual's sensitivities, with the resulting loss of the objectivity that can draw strength from seeking the causes of things. But it is exactly Miss Cather's point that the Lucretian *rerum natura* means little; an admirer of Virgil, she is content with the *lacrimae rerum,* the tears for things.

Miss Cather's later books are pervaded by the air of a brooding ancient wisdom, but if we examine her mystical concern with pots and pans, it does not seem much more than an oblique defense of gentility or very far from the gaudy domesticity of bourgeois accumulation glorified in the *Woman's Home Companion.* And with it goes a culture-snobbery and even a caste-snobbery. The Willa Cather of the older days shared the old racial democracy of the West. It is strange to find the Willa Cather of the present talking about "the adopted American," the young man of German, Jewish or Scandinavian descent who can never appreciate Sarah Orne Jewett and for whom American English can never be more than a means of communicating ideas: "It is surface speech: he clicks the words out as a bank clerk clicks out silver when you ask for change. For him the language has no emotional roots." This is indeed the gentility of Katherine Fullerton Gerould, and in large part the result, one suspects, of what Parrington calls "the inferiority complex of the frontier mind before the old and established."

Yet the place to look for the whole implications of a writer's philosophy is in the esthetic of his work. *Lucy Gayheart* shows to the full the effect of Miss Cather's point of view. It has always been a personal failure of her talent that prevented her from involving her people in truly dramatic relations with each other. (Her women, for example, always stand in the mother or daughter relation to men; they are never truly lovers.) But at least once upon a time her people were involved in a dramatic relation with themselves or with their environments, whereas now *Lucy Gayheart* has not even this involvement. Environment does not exist, fate springs from nothing save chance; the characters are unattached to anything save their dreams. The novel has been *démeublé* indeed; but life without its furniture is strangely bare.

Irony with a Center:
Katherine Anne Porter

by Robert Penn Warren

The fiction of Katherine Anne Porter, despite widespread critical adulation, has never found the public which its distinction merits. Many of her stories are unsurpassed in modern fiction, and some are not often equaled. She belongs to the relatively small group of writers—extraordinarily small, when one considers the vast number of stories published every year in English and American magazines—who have done serious, consistent, original, and vital work in the form of short fiction—the group which would include James Joyce, Katherine Mansfield, Sherwood Anderson, and Ernest Hemingway. This list does not include a considerable number of other writers who, though often finding other forms more congenial—the novel or poetry—have scored occasional triumphs in the field of short fiction. Then, of course, there is a very large group of writers who have a great facility, a great mechanical competence, and sometimes moments of real perception, but who work from no fundamental and central conviction.

It was once fashionable to argue complacently that the popular magazine had created the short story—had provided the market and had cultivated an appetite for the product. It is true that the magazine did provide the market, but at the same time, and progressively, the magazine has corrupted the short story. What the magazine encourages is not so much the short story as a conscious or unconscious division of the artistic self of the writer. One can still discover (as in an address delivered by Mr. Frederick Lewis Allen to the American Philosophical Society) a genial self-congratulation in the face of "mass appreciation." But, writes Mr. R. P. Blackmur in reply:

> In fact, mass appreciation of the kind which Mr. Allen approves represents the constant danger to the artist of any serious sort: the danger of popularization *before* creation. ... The difference between great art and popular art is relatively small; but the difference between either and popularized art is radical, and absolute. Popular art is topical and natural, great art is deliberate and thematic. What can be popularized in either is only what can be sold...a scheme which requires the constant replacement of the shoddy goods. He (Mr. Allen) does not mean to avow this; he no doubt means the contrary; but there it is. Until American or any other society is educated either up to the level or back to the level of art with standards, whether popular or great, it can be sold nothing but art without standards. ...

The fact that Miss Porter has not attempted a compromise may account for the relatively small body of her published fiction. There was the collection of stories published in 1931 under the title *Flowering Judas;* an enlarged collection, under the same title in 1935, which includes two novelettes, *The Cracked Looking-Glass* and *Hacienda,* the latter of which had been previously published by Harrison, in Paris; a collection of three novelettes under the title *Pale Horse, Pale Rider,* in 1939; the Modern Library edition of *Flowering Judas;* and a few pieces, not yet in book form, which have appeared in various magazines—for instance, sections of the uncompleted biography of Cotton Mather and the brilliant story "A Day's Work."[1]

Her method of composition does not, in itself, bend readily to the compromise. In many instances, a story or novelette has not been composed straight off. Instead, a section here and a section there have been written—little germinal scenes explored and developed. Or scenes or sketches of character which were never intended to be incorporated in the finished work have been developed in the process of trying to understand the full potentiality of the material. One might guess at an approach something like this: a special, local excitement provoked by the material—character or incident; an attempt to define the nature of that local

[1]Since included in the volume *The Leaning Tower.*

excitement, as local—to squeeze it and not lose a drop; an attempt to understand the relationships of the local excitements and to define the implications—to arrive at theme; the struggle to reduce theme to pattern. That would seem to be the natural history of the characteristic story. Certainly, it is a method which requires time, scrupulosity, and contemplation.

The method itself is an index to the characteristics of Miss Porter's fiction—the rich surface detail scattered with apparently casual profuseness and the close structure which makes such detail meaningful; the great compression and economy which one discovers upon analysis; the precision of psychology and observation, the texture of the style.

Most reviewers, commenting upon Miss Porter's distinction, refer to her "style"—struck, no doubt, by an exceptional felicity of phrase, a precision in the use of metaphor, and a subtlety of rhythm. It is not only the appreciation of the obviously poetical strain in Miss Porter's work that has tended to give her reputation some flavor of the special and exquisite, but also the appreciation of the exceptional precision of her language. When one eminent critic praises her for an "English of a purity and precision almost unique in contemporary American fiction," he is giving praise richly merited and praise for a most important quality, but this praise, sad to relate as a commentary on our times, is a kind that does encourage the special reputation. This same eminent critic also praises Miss Porter as an artist, which goes to say that he himself knows very well that her language is but one aspect of her creations; but even so, the word *artist* carries its own overtones of exquisiteness.

The heart of the potential reader may have been chilled—and I believe quite rightly—by the praise of "beautiful style." He is put off by a reviewer's easy abstracting of style for comment and praise; his innocence repudiates the fallacy of agreeable style. The famous common reader is not much concerned with English as such, pure or impure, precise or imprecise, and he is no more concerned with the artist as artist. He is concerned with what the English will say to him, and with what the artist will do for him, or to him.

It is, of course, just and proper for us to praise Miss Porter for her English and her artistry, but we should remind ourselves that we prize those things because she uses them to create vivid and significant images of life. All this is not to say that we are taking the easy moralistic, or easy Philistine, view of English or artistry. We know that the vividness and the significance of any literary work exist only in the proper medium, and that only because of a feeling for the medium and an understanding of artistry did the writer succeed, in the first place, in discovering vividness and significance. We hope that we shall never have to remind ourselves of that fact, and now we remind ourselves of the vividness and significance in which Miss Porter's English and artistry eventuate, only because we would balance praise for the special with praise for the general, praise for subtlety with praise for strength, praise for sensibility with praise for intellect.

But let us linger upon the matter of Miss Porter's style in the hope that it can be used as a point of departure. Take, for example, a paragraph from the title story of *Flowering Judas,* the description of Braggioni, the half-Italian, half-Indian revolutionist in Mexico, "a leader of men, skilled revolutionist, and his skin has been punctured in honorable warfare." His followers "warm themselves in his reflected glory and say to each other, 'He has a real nobility, a love of humanity raised above mere personal affections.' The excess of this self-love has flowed out, inconveniently for her, over Laura"—the puzzled American girl who has been lured to Mexico by revolutionary enthusiasm and before whom he sits with his guitar and sings sentimental songs, while his wife weeps at home. But here is the passage.

> Braggioni...leans forward, balancing his paunch between his spread knees, and sings with tremendous emphasis, weighing his words. He has, the song relates, no father and no mother, nor even a friend to console him; lonely as a wave of the sea he comes and goes, lonely as a wave. His mouth opens round and yearns sideways, his balloon cheeks grow oily with the labor of song. He bulges marvelously in his expensive garments. Over his lavender collar, crushed upon a purple necktie, held by a diamond hoop: over his ammunition belt of tooled leather worked in silver, buckled cruelly around his gasping middle: over the tops of his glossy yellow shoes Braggioni swells with ominous ripeness, his mauve silk hose stretched taut, his ankles bound with the stout leather thongs of his shoes.
>
> When he stretches his eyelids at Laura she notes again that his eyes are the true tawny yellow cat's eyes. He is rich, not in money,

he tells her, but in power, and this power brings with it the blameless ownership of things, and the right to indulge his love of small
luxuries. "I have a taste for the elegant refinements," he said once,
flourishing a yellow silk handkerchief before her nose. "Smell
that? It is Jockey Club, imported from New York." Nonetheless he
is wounded by life. He will say so presently. "It is true everything
turns to dust in the hand, to gall on the tongue." He sighs and his
leather belt creaks like a saddle girth.

The passage is sharp and evocative. Its phrasing embodies a
mixture, a fusion, of the shock of surprise and the satisfaction of
precision—a resolved tension, which may do much to account for
the resonance and vibration of the passage. We have in it the statement, "His mouth opens round and yearns sideways"—and we
note the two words *yearns* and *sideways;* in the phrase, "labor of
song"; in, "he bulges marvelously"; in, "Braggioni swells with
ominous ripeness." But upon inspection it may be discovered that
the effect of these details is not merely a local effect. The subtle
local evocations really involve us in the center of the scene; we
are taken to the core of the meaning of the scene, and thence to
the central impulse of the story; and thence, possibly to the germinal idea of all of this author's fiction. All of these filaments
cannot be pursued back through the web—the occasion does not
permit; but perhaps a few can be traced to the meaning of the
scene itself in the story.

What we have here is the revolutionist who loves luxury, who
feels that power gives blameless justification to the love of elegant refinements, but whose skin has been punctured in "honorable warfare"; who is a competent leader of men, but who is vain
and indolent; who is sentimental and self-pitying, but, at the same
time, ruthless; who betrays his wife and yet, upon his return
home, will weep with his wife as she washes his feet and weeps;
who labors for the good of man, but is filled with self-love.

We have here a tissue of contradictions, and the very phraseol-
ogy takes us to these contradictions. For instance, the word *yearns*
involves the sentimental, blurred emotion, but immediately
afterward the words *sideways* and *oily* remind us of the grossness, the brutality, the physical appetite. So with the implied
paradox in the "labor of song." The ammunition belt, we recall,
is buckled *cruelly* about his "gasping middle." The ammunition

belt reminds us that this indolent, fat, apparently soft, vain man is capable of violent action, is a man of violent profession, and sets the stage for the word *cruelly,* which involves the paradox of the man who loves mankind and is capable of individual cruelties, and which, further, reminds us that he punishes himself out of physical vanity and punishes himself by defining himself in his calling—the only thing that belts in his sprawling, meaningless animality. He swells with "ominous ripeness"—and we sense the violent threat in the man as contrasted with his softness, a kind of great overripe plum as dangerous as a grenade, a feeling of corruption mixed with sentimental sweetness; and specifically we are reminded of the threat to Laura in the situation. We come to the phrase "wounded by life," and we pick up again the motif hinted at in the song and in the lingering rhythms: "He has, the song relates, no father and no mother, nor even a friend to console him; lonely as a wave of the sea he comes and goes, lonely as a wave." In nothing is there to be found a balm—not in revolution, in vanity, in love—for the "vast cureless wound of his self-esteem." Then, after the bit about the wound, we find the sentence: "He sighs and his leather belt creaks like a saddle girth." The defeated, sentimental sigh, the cureless wound, and the bestial creaking of the leather.

If this reading of the passage is acceptable, the passage itself is a rendering of the problem which the character of Braggioni poses to Laura. It is stated, in bare, synoptic form, elsewhere:

> The gluttonous bulk of Braggioni has become a symbol of her many disillusions, for a revolutionist should be lean, animated by heroic faith, a vessel of abstract virtues. This is nonsense, she knows it now and is ashamed of it. Revolution must have leaders, and leadership is a career for energetic men. She is, her comrades tell her, full of romantic error, for what she defines as a cynicism is to them merely a developed sense of reality.

What is the moral reality here? This question is, I should say, the theme of the story, which exists in an intricate tissue of paradox, and is posed only in the dream Laura has at the end, a dream which embodies but does not resolve the question.

With all the enchanting glitter of style and all the purity of language and all the flow and flicker of feeling, Miss Porter's imagination, as a matter of fact, is best appreciated if we appreciate its essential austerity, its devotion to the fact drenched in God's direct daylight, its concern with the inwardness of character, and its delight in the rigorous and discriminating deployment of a theme. Let us take another passage from her work, a passage from the novelette *Noon Wine,* the description of Mr. Thompson, a poor dirt-farmer in Texas, busy at his churning, a task that he, in his masculine pride and bitter incompetence, finds contemptible and demeaning:

> Mr. Thompson was a tough weather-beaten man with stiff black hair and a week's growth of black whiskers. He was a noisy proud man who held his neck so straight his whole face stood level with his Adam's apple, and the whiskers continued down his neck and disappeared into a black thatch under his open collar. The churn rumbled and swished like the belly of a trotting horse, and Mr. Thompson seemed somehow to be driving a horse with one hand, reining it in and urging it forward; and every now and then he turned halfway around and squirted a tremendous spit of tobacco juice out over the steps. The door stones were brown and gleaming with fresh tobacco juice.

This passage is simple and unpretending, a casual introductory description near the beginning of a story, but it succeeds in having its own kind of glitter and purity and flow. Here those things come, as in so much of Miss Porter's fiction, from the writer's rigorous repudiation of obvious literary resources, resources which, on other occasions, she can use so brilliantly. The things that stir our admiration in the passage from "Flowering Judas" are notably absent here, are notably eschewed. Here the style is of the utmost transparency, and our eye and ear are captivated by the very ordinariness of the ordinary items presented to us, the trotting motion of the churn, the swish of the milk, the tobacco juice glittering on the door stones. Miss Porter has the power of isolating common things, the power that Chekhov or Frost or Ibsen or, sometimes, Pound has, the power to make the common thing glow with an Eden-innocence by the mere fact of the isolation. It is a kind of indicative poetry.

Miss Porter's eye and ear, however, do not seize with merely random and innocent delight on the objects of the world, even though we may take that kind of delight in the objects she so lovingly places before us, transmuted in their ordinariness. If the

fact drenched in daylight commands her unfaltering devotion, it
is because such facts are in themselves a deep language, or can be
made to utter a language of the deepest burden. What are the simple facts saying in the paragraph just quoted?

They are saying something about Mr. Thompson, poor Mr.
Thompson who will die of a self-inflicted gunshot wound before
many pages have passed, and will die of it because he is all the
things we might have surmised of him if we had been able to
understand beforehand the language of the simple facts of the
scene at the churn. The pridefully stiff neck and the black whisk-
ers, they tell us something. He is the sort of man who ought, or
thinks he ought, to be holding the reins of a spanking horse and
not the cord of a churn, and his very gesture has a kind of childish
play acting. Somewhere in his deepest being, he is reminded of
the spanking horse with the belly swishing in the trot, the horse
such a fine manly man ought to have under his hand, if luck just
weren't so ornery and unreasonable, and so he plays the game
with himself. But he can't quite convince himself. It is only a poor
old churn, after all, woman's work on a rundown and debt-bit
shirt-tail farm, with kids and an ailing wife, and so he spits his
tremendous spits of masculine protest against fate, and the brown
juice gleams with its silly, innocent assertiveness on the stones the
woman's broom has, so many times, swept clean of this and that.
In the end, looking back, we can see that the story is the story of a
noisy, proud, stiff-necked man whose pride has constantly suffered under failure, who salves his hurt pride by harmless bluster
with his wife and children, and who, in the end, stumbles into a
situation which takes the last prop of certainty from his life.

Our first glimpse of Mrs. Thompson is in the "front room,"
where she lies with the green shade down and a wet cloth over her
poor weak eyes. But in spite of the weeping eyes, the longing for
the cool dark, and all her sad incompetence, on the one hand,
and Mr. Thompson's bluster and hurt pride on the other, there is
a warm secret life between them:

> "Tell *you* the truth, Ellie," said Mr. Thompson, picking his teeth
> with a fork and leaning back in the best of humors, "I always
> thought your granma was a ter'ble ole fool. She'd just say the first
> thing that popped into her head and call it God's wisdom."
>
> "My granma wasn't anybody's fool. Nine times out of ten she

knew what she was talking about. I always say, the first thing you think is the best thing you can say."

"Well," said Mr. Thompson, going into another shout, "you're so *ree*fined about that goat story, you just try speaking out in mixed comp'ny sometime! You just try it. S'pose you happened to be thinking about a hen and a rooster, hey? I reckon you'd shock the Babtist preacher!" He gave her a good pinch on her thin little rump. "No more meat on you than a rabbit," he said, fondly. "Now I like 'em cornfed."

Mrs. Thompson looked at him open-eyed and blushed. She could see better by lamplight. "Why, Mr. Thompson, sometimes I think you're the evilest-minded man that ever lived." She took a handful of hair on the crown of his head and gave it a good, slow pull. "That's to show you how it feels, pinching so hard when you're supposed to be playing," she said, gently.

This little glimpse of their secret life, Mr. Thompson's masculine, affectionate bragging and bullying and teasing, and Mrs. Thompson's shy and embarrassed playfulness, comes as a surprise in the middle of their drab world, a sudden brightness and warmth. Without this episode we should never get the full force of Mr. Thompson's bafflement and anger when Mr. Hatch, the baleful stranger, misinterprets Mr. Thompson's prideful talk of his wife's ill health and says that he himself would get rid of a puny wife mighty quick. And without this episode we should never sense how that bafflement and anger flow, as one more component, into the moment when Mr. Thompson sees, or thinks he sees, the blade of Mr. Hatch's bowie knife go into the poor Swede's stomach, and he brings his axe down on Hatch's head, as though stunning a beef.

We are, however, getting ahead of ourselves. Let us summarize the apparently simple story. On Mr. Thompson's poverty-bit farm a stranger appears, a Swede, Mr. Helton, who takes work at a low wage, plays the harmonica in his off hours, and seems to inhabit some vague and lonely inner world. But Mr. Helton is a worker, and for the first time the farm begins to pay. Mr. Thompson can give up "woman's work," can do the big important things that become a man, and can bask in the new prosperity. Nine years later, to interrupt the new prosperity, another stranger appears, a Mr. Hatch, who reveals that the Swede is a murderer and a lunatic whom he will arrest and take back North to the asylum.

When the Swede appears, Mr. Thompson sees, or thinks he sees, Mr. Hatch's knife going into his stomach. With his axe he kills Mr. Hatch, defending the Swede, defending what, he does not know.

After the deed, there isn't, strangely enough, a scratch on the Swede's stomach. This doesn't bother the jury, and Mr. Thompson is acquitted in no time at all. But it does bother Mr. Thompson. He simply can't understand things, how he could see the knife go in and then find it not true, and all the other things he can't understand. He had never intended to do it, he was just protecting the poor Swede. But we are aware that there had been the slow building up of the mysterious anger against Mr. Hatch, of the fear that Mr. Hatch threatened the new prosperity of the farm. And in the trial Mr. Thompson has been caught in a web of little lies, small distortions of fact, nothing serious, nothing needed to prove he wasn't guilty, just little twists to make everything clearer and simpler.

Is Mr. Thompson innocent or guilty? He doesn't really know. Caught in the mysteriousness of himself, caught in all the impulses which he had never been able to face, caught in all the little lies which had really meant no harm, he can't know the truth about anything. He can't stand the moral uncertainty of this situation, but he does not know what it is that most deeply he can't stand. He can't stand not knowing what he himself really is. His pride can't stand that kind of nothingness. Not knowing what it is he can't stand, he is under the compulsion to go, day after day, around the countryside, explaining himself, explaining how he had not meant to do it, how it was defense of the Swede, how it was self-defense, all the while plunging deeper and deeper into the morass of his fate. Then he finds that his own family have, all along, thought him guilty. So the proud man has to kill himself to prove, in his last pride, that he is really innocent.

That, however, is the one thing that can never be proved, for the story is about the difficult definition of guilt and innocence. Mr. Thompson, not able to trust his own innocence, or understand the nature of whatever guilt is his, has taken refuge in the lie, and the lie, in the end, kills him. The issue here, as in "Flowering Judas," is not to be decided simply. It is, in a sense, left suspended, the terms defined, but the argument left only at a provisional resolution. Poor Mr. Thompson—innocent and yet guilty, and in his pride unable to live by the provisional.

The Cracked Looking-Glass, too, is about guilt and innocence. It is the story of a high-spirited, pleasure-loving Irish girl, married to a much older man, faithful to him, yet needing the society of young fun-provoking men, to whom she takes a motherly or sisterly attitude. She lives a kind of lie—in fact, she can't tell anything without giving it a romantic embroidery. Then she is horrified to discover that her Connecticut neighbors think her a bad woman, suspect her of infidelities. At the end, sitting in her tight kitchen with Old Dennis, "while beyond were far off places full of life and gaiety...and beyond everything like a green field with morning sun on it lay youth and Ireland," she leans over and puts her hand on her husband's knee, and asks him, in an ordinary voice: "Whyever did ye marry a woman like me?"

Dennis says mind, she doesn't tip the chair over, and adds that he knew he could never do better. Then:

> She sat up and felt his sleeves carefully. "I want you to wrap up warm this bitter weather, Dennis," she told him. "With two pairs of socks and the chest protector, for if anything happened to you, whatever would become of me in this world?"
>
> "Let's not think of it," said Dennis, shuffling his feet.
>
> "Let's not, then," said Rosaleen. "For I could cry if you crooked a finger at me."

Again the provisional resolution of the forces of the story: not a solution which Rosaleen can live by with surety, but one which she must re-learn and re-earn every day.

With the theme of *The Cracked Looking-Glass* in mind, let us take another of the novelettes, *Old Mortality.*

To begin, *Old Mortality* is relatively short, some twenty thousand words, but it gives an impression of the mass of a novel. One factor contributing to this effect is the length of the time span; the novelette falls into three sections, dated 1885-1902, 1904, and 1912. Another factor is the considerable number of the characters, who, despite the brevity of the story, are sketched in with great precision; we know little about them, but that little means much. Another, and not quite so obvious but perhaps more important, factor is the rich circumstantiality and easy discursiveness, especially in Part I, which sets the tone of the piece. The author lingers on anecdote, apparently just to relish the anecdote, to extract the humor or pathos—but in the end we discover that there has been no casual self-indulgence, or indulgence of the reader; the details of the easy anecdote, which seemed to exist at the moment for itself alone, have been working busily in the cellarage of our minds.

Part I, 1885-1902, introduces us to two little girls, Maria and Miranda, aged twelve and eight, through whose eyes we see the family. There is the grandmother, who takes no part in the action of the story, but whose brief characterization, we discover, is important—the old lady who, "twice a year compelled in her blood by the change of seasons, would sit nearly all day beside old trunks and boxes in the lumber room, unfolding layers of garments and small keepsakes... unwrapping locks of hair and dried flowers, crying gently and easily as if tears were the only pleasure she had left." (Her piety—stirred by the equinoxes, as unreflecting as tropism—provides the basic contrast for the end of the story; her piety does not achieve the form of legend—merely a compulsion of the blood, the focus of old affections.) There is the father, "a pleasant everyday sort of man"—who once shot to protect the family "honor" and had to run to Mexico. There is Cousin Eva, chinless and unbeautiful amidst the belles, who, when we first meet her, teaches Latin in a female seminary and tries to interest Maria and Miranda in that study by telling them the story of John Wilkes Booth, "who, handsomely garbed in a long black cloak"—so the story is recast by the little girls—"had leaped to the stage after assassinating President Lincoln. 'Sic semper tyrannis,' he had shouted superbly, in spite of his broken leg." There is Amy, dead, already a legend, a beautiful sad family story, the girl who almost had a duel fought over her in New Orleans, who drove her suitor, Cousin Gabriel, almost to distraction before she married him, and who died under mysterious circumstances a few weeks after her marriage. There is Gabriel himself, fond of the races, cut off by his grandfather without a penny, a victim of the bottle in his bereavement; he marries Miss Honey, who can never compete with the legend of the dead Amy. In this section, the little girls attempt to make the people they know and the stories they have heard fit together, make sense; and always at the center is the story of Amy.

Part II, in contrast with Part I with its discursiveness, its blurring of time, its anecdotal richness, gives a single fully developed scene, dated 1904. The father takes the little girls, on holiday from their convent school, to the races. There, out of family piety, they bet their dollar on Uncle Gabriel's horse—a poor hundred-to-one shot. (Piety and common sense—they know even at their tender years that a hundred-to-one bet is no bet at all—are in conflict, and piety wins only because of the father's pressure.) But Gabriel's horse comes in, and they see for the first time their romantic Uncle Gabriel—"a shabby fat man with blood-shot blue eyes...and a big melancholy laugh like a groan"—now drunk, and after his victory, weeping. But he takes them to meet Miss Honey, Amy's successor, in his shabby apartment, and the little girls know that Miss Honey hates them all.

Part III, 1912, shows us Miranda on a train going to the funeral of Uncle Gabriel, who has died in Lexington, Kentucky, but has been brought home to lie beside Amy—to whom he belongs. On the train Miranda, now a young lady recently married, meets Cousin Eva, whom she has not seen for many years, who has, since the days at the seminary, crusaded for woman suffrage and gone to jail for her convictions. The talk goes back to the family story, to Amy. "Everybody loved Amy," Miranda remarks, but Cousin Eva replies: "Not everybody by a long shot. ... She had enemies. If she knew she pretended she didn't. ... She was sweet as honeycomb to everybody. ... That was the trouble. She went through life like a spoiled darling, doing as she pleased and letting other people suffer for it." Then: "'I never believed for one moment,' says Cousin Eva, putting her mouth close to Miranda's ear and breathing peppermint hotly into it, 'that Amy was an impure woman. Never! But let me tell you there were plenty who did believe it.'" So Cousin Eva begins to reinterpret the past, all the romantic past, the legend of Amy, who, according to Cousin Eva, was not beautiful, just good-looking, whose illness hadn't been romantic, and who had, she says, committed suicide.

Cousin Eva defines the bitter rivalry under the gaiety of the legend, the vicious competition among the belles. And more:

Cousin Eva wrung her hands. "It was just sex," she said in despair; [The word *despair,* caught in the frustrated and yet victorious old woman's casual gesture, is important—a resonance from her per-

sonal story which gives an echo to the theme of the story itself.]
"their minds dwelt on nothing else. They didn't call it that, it
was all smothered under pretty names, but that's all it was, sex."

So Cousin Eva, who has given her life to learning and a progres-
sive cause, defines all the legend in terms of economics and biology. "They simply festered inside," she says of all the Amys,
"they festered."

But Miranda, catching a Baudelairean vision of "corruption
concealed under lace and flowers," thinks quite coldly: "Of
course, it was not like that. This is no more true than what I was
told before, it's every bit as romantic." And in revulsion from
Cousin Eva, she wants to get home, though she is grown and married now, and see her father and sister, who are solid and alive,
are not merely "definitions."

But when she arrives her father cannot take her in, in the old
way. He turns to Cousin Eva. And the two old people, who represent the competing views of the past—love and poetry opposed to
biology and economics—sit down together in a world, their world
of the past, which excludes Miranda. Miranda thinks: "Where are
my own people and my own time?" She thinks, and the thought
concludes the story: "Let them go on explaining how things happened. I don't care. At least I can know the truth about what
happens to me, she assured herself silently, making a promise to
herself, in her hopefulness, her ignorance."

So much for the action of the story. We see immediately that it
is a story about legend, and it is an easy extension to the symbol
for tradition, the meaning of the past for the present. We gradually become acquainted with the particular legend through the little
girls, but the little girls themselves, in their innocence, criticize
the legend. Their father, speaking of Amy's slimness, for instance, says: "There were never any fat women in the family,
thank God." But the little girls remember Aunt Keziah, in Kentucky, who was famous for her heft. (Such an anecdote is developed richly and humorously, with no obvious pointing to the
theme, beyond the logic of the context.) Such details, in Part I,
develop the first criticism of the legend, the criticism by innocent
common sense. In Part II, the contrast between Gabriel as legend
and Gabriel as real extends the same type of criticism, but more
dramatically; but here another, a moral criticism, enters in, for

we have the effect of Amy on other people's lives, on Gabriel and Miss Honey. This, however, is not specified; it merely charges the scene of the meeting between Miranda and Cousin Eva on the way to Gabriel's funeral. Part III at first gives us, in Cousin Eva's words, the modern critical method applied to the legend — as if invoking Marx and Freud.

Up to this point, the line of the story has been developed fairly directly, though under a complicated surface. The story could end here, a story of repudiation, and some readers have interpreted it as such. But — and here comes the first reversal of the field — Miranda repudiates Cousin Eva's version, as romantic, too, in favor of the "reality" of her father, whom she is soon to see. But there is another shift. Miranda discovers that she is cut off from her father, who turns to Cousin Eva, whose "myth" contradicts his "myth," but whose world he can share. Miranda, cut off, determines to leave them to their own sterile pursuit of trying to understand the past. She will understand herself, the truth of what happens to her. This would provide another point of rest for the story — a story about the brave younger generation, their hope, courage, and honesty, and some readers have taken it thus. But — withheld cunningly until the end, until the last few words — there is a last reversal of the field. Miranda makes her promise to herself in "her hopefulness, her ignorance." And those two words, *hopefulness, ignorance,* suddenly echo throughout the story.

Miranda will find *a* truth, as it were, but it, too, will be a myth, for it will not be translatable, or, finally, communicable. But it will be the only truth she can win, and for better or worse she will have to live by it. She must live by her own myth. But she must earn her myth in the process of living. Her myth will be a new myth, different from the mutually competing myths of her father and Cousin Eva, but stemming from that antinomy. Those competing myths will simply provide the terms of her own dialectic of living.

We remember that the heroine's name is Miranda, and we may remember Miranda of Shakespeare's *Tempest,* who exclaims, "O brave new world, that has such people in it!" Perhaps the identity of the name is not an accident. Miranda of *Old Mortality* has passed a step beyond that moment of that exclamation, but she, too, has seen the pageant raised by Prospero's wand — the pageant evoked by her father, the pleasant everyday sort of father, who, however, is a Prospero, though lacking the other Prospero's irony. For *Old Mortality*, like *The Tempest*, is about illusion and reality, and comes to rest upon a perilous irony.

In *Old Mortality* Miss Porter has used very conventional materials; the conventional materials, however, are revitalized by the intellectual scope of the interpretation and the precision and subtlety of structure. But Miss Porter has not committed herself to one type of material. The world of balls and horsemanship and romance is exchanged in *Noon Wine*, as we have seen, for a poverty-ridden Texas farm; in *Pale Horse, Pale Rider*, for a newspaper office and a rooming house at the time of World War I; in "Hacienda," "Flowering Judas" and "María Concepción," for Mexico. We may ask, What is the common denominator of these stories, aside from the obvious similarities of style (though the style itself is very flexible)? What is the central "view," the central intuition?

In these stories, and, as I believe, in many others, there is the same paradoxical problem of definition, the same delicate balancing of rival considerations, the same scrupulous development of competing claims to attention and action, the same interplay of the humorous and the serious, the same refusal to take the straight line, the formula, through the material at hand. This has implied for some readers that the underlying attitude is one of skepticism, negation, refusal to confront the need for immediate, watertight, foolproof solutions. The skeptical and ironical bias is, I think, important in Miss Porter's work, and it is true that her work wears an air of detachment and contemplation. But, I should say, her irony is an irony with a center, never an irony for irony's sake. It simply implies, I think, a refusal to accept the formula, the ready-made solution, the hand-me-down morality, the word for the spirit. It affirms, rather, the constant need for exercising discrimination, the arduous obligation of the intellect in the face of conflicting dogmas, the need for a dialectical approach to matters of definition, the need for exercising as much of the human faculty as possible.

This basic attitude finds its correlation in her work, in the delicacy of phrase, the close structure, the counterpoint of incident and implication. That is, a story must test its thematic line at every point against its total circumstantiality; the thematic considerations must, as it were, be validated in terms of circum-stance and experience, and never be resolved in the poverty of statement.

In one sense, it is the intellectual rigor and discrimination that gives Miss Porter's work its classic distinction and control—that is, if any one quality can be said to be uniquely responsible. No, no single quality can take that credit, but where many writers have achieved stories of perception, feeling, sensibility, strength, or charm, few have been able to achieve stories of a deep philo-sophic urgency in the narrow space, and fewer still have been able to achieve the kind of thematic integration of a body of stories, the mark of the masters, the thing that makes us think first of the central significance of a writer rather than of some incidental and individual triumph. For Miss Porter's bright indicative poetry is, at long last, a literally metaphysical poetry, too. The luminosity is from inward.

The Eye of the Story

by Eudora Welty

In "Old Mortality" how stirring the horse race is! At the finish the crowd breaks into its long roar "like the falling walls of Jericho." This we hear, and it is almost like seeing, and we know Miss Lucy has won. But beyond a fleeting glimpse—the "mahogany streak" of Miss Lucy on the track—we never get much sight of the race with our eyes. What we see comes afterward. Then we have it up close: Miss Lucy bleeding at the nose. For Miranda has got to say "That's winning too." The race would never have got into the story except that Miranda's heart is being prepared to reject victory, to reject the glamor of the race and the cheering grandstand; to distrust from now on all evidence except what she, out of her own experience, can testify to. By the time we *see* Miss Lucy, she is a sight for Miranda's eyes alone: as much symbol as horse.

Most good stories are about the interior of our lives, but Katherine Anne Porter's stories take place there; they show surface only at her choosing. Her use of the physical world is enough to meet her needs and no more; she is not wasteful with anything. This artist, writing her stories with a power that stamps them to their last detail on the memory, does so to an extraordinary degree without sensory imagery.

I have the most common type of mind, the visual, and when first I began to read her stories it stood in the way of my trust in my own certainty of what was there that, for all my being bowled over by them, I couldn't see them happening. This was a very good thing for me. As her work has done in many other respects, it has shown me a thing or two about the eye of fiction, about fiction's visibility and invisibility, about its clarity, its radiance.

Heaven knows she can see. Katherine Anne Porter has seen all her life, sees today, most intimately, most specifically, and down to the bones, and she could date the bones. There is, above all, "Noon Wine" to establish it forever that when she wants a story to be visible, it is. "Noon Wine" is visible all the way through, full of scenes charged with dramatic energy; everything is brought forth into movement, dialogue; the title itself is Mr. Helton's tune on the harmonica. "Noon Wine" is the most beautifully objective work she has done. And nothing has been sacrificed to its being so (or she wouldn't have done it); to the contrary. I find Mr. Hatch the scariest character she ever made, and he's just set down there in Texas, like a chair. There he stands, part of the everyday furniture of living. He's opaque, and he's the devil. Walking in at Mr. Thompson's gate—the same gate by which his tracked-down victim walked in first—he is that much more horrifying, almost too solid to the eyes to be countenanced. (So much for the visual mind.)

Katherine Anne Porter has not in general chosen to cast her stories in scenes. Her sense of human encounter is profound, is fundamental to her work, I believe, but she has not often allowed it the dramatic character it takes in "Noon Wine." We may not see the significant moment happen within the story's present; we may not watch it occur between the two characters it joins. Instead, a silent blow falls while one character is alone—the most alone in his life, perhaps. (And this is the case in "Noon Wine" too.) Often the revelation that pierces a character's mind and heart and shows him his life or his death comes in a dream, in retrospect, in illness or in utter defeat, the moment of vanishing hope, the moment of dying. What Miss Porter makes us see are those subjective worlds of hallucination, obsession, fever, guilt. The presence of death hovering about Granny Weatherall she makes as real and brings as near as Granny's own familiar room that stands about her bed—realer, nearer, for we recognize not only death's presence but the character death has come in for Granny Weatherall.

The flash of revelation is revelation but is unshared. But how unsuspecting we are to imagine so for a moment—it *is* shared, and by ourselves, her readers, who must share it feeling the doubled anguish of knowing this fact, doubled still again when it is borne in upon us how close to life this is, to *our* lives.

It is to be remembered that the world of fiction is not of itself visible. A story may or may not be born in sensory images in a given writer's mind. Experience itself is stored in no telling how many ways in a writer's memory. (It was "the sound of the sea, and Beryl fanning her hair at the window" that years later and thousands of miles away brought Katherine Mansfield to writing "At the Bay.") But if the physical world *is* visible or audible in the story, it has to be made so. Its materialization is as much a created thing as are the story's characters and what they think or do or say.

Katherine Anne Porter shows us that we do not have to see a story happen to know what is taking place. For all we are to know, she is not looking at it happen herself when she writes it; for her eyes are always looking through the gauze of the passing scene, not distracted by the immediate and transitory; her vision is reflective.

Her imagery is as likely as not to belong to a time other than the story's present, and beyond that it always differs from it in nature; it is *memory* imagery, coming into the story from memory's remove. It is a distilled, a re-formed imagery, for it is part of a language made to speak directly of premonition, warning, surmise, anger, despair.

It was soon borne in upon me that Katherine Anne Porter's moral convictions have given her readers another way to see. Surely these convictions represent the fixed points about which her work has turned, and not only that but they govern her stories down to the smallest detail. Her work has formed a constellation, with its own North Star.

Is the writer who does not give us the pictures and bring us the sounds of a story as it unfolds shutting out part of life? In Katherine Anne Porter's stories the effect has surely been never to diminish life but always to intensify life in the part significant to her story. It is a darkening of the house as the curtain goes up on this stage of her own.

Her stories of Mexico, Germany, Texas all happen there: where love and hate, trust and betrayal happen. And so their author's gaze is turned not outward but inward, and has confronted the mysterious dark from her work's beginning.

Since her subject is what lies beneath the surface, her way—quite direct—is to penetrate, brush the stuff away. It is the writer like Chekov whose way of working is indirect. He moved indeed toward the same heart and core but by building up some corresponding illusion of life. Writers of Chekov's side of the family are themselves illusionists and have necessarily a certain fondness for, lenience toward, the whole shimmering fabric as such. Here we have the professional scientist, the good doctor, working with illusion and the born romantic artist—is she not?—working without it. Perhaps it is always the lyrical spirit that takes on instantaneous color, shape, pattern of motion in work, while the meditative spirit must fly as quickly as possible out of the shell.

All the stories she has written are moral stories about love and the hate that is love's twin, love's impostor and enemy and death. Rejection, betrayal, desertion, theft roam the pages of her stories as they roam the world. The madam kicking the girl in "Magic" and the rest of the brutality in the characters' treatment of one another; the thieving that in one form or another infects their relationships; the protests they make, from the weakness of false dreams or of lying down with a cold cloth over the eyes, on up to towering rages: all this is a way of showing to the inward eye: Look at what you are doing to human love.

We hear in how many more stories than the one the litany of the little boy at the end of "The Downward Path to Wisdom," his "comfortable, sleepy song": "I hate Papa, I hate Mama, I hate Grandma, I hate Uncle David, I hate Old Janet, I hate Marjory, I hate Papa, I hate Mama. ...." It is like the long list of remembered losses in the story "Theft" made vocal, and we remember how that loser's decision to go on and let herself be robbed coincides with the rising "in her blood" of "a deep almost murderous anger."

"If one is afraid of looking into a face one hits the face," remarked W. B. Yeats, and I think we must conclude that to Katherine Anne Porter's characters this face is the challenging face of love itself. And I think it is the faces—the inner, secret faces—of her characters, in their self-delusion, their venom and pain, that their author herself is contemplating. More than either looking at the face or hitting it, she has made a story out of her anger.

If outrage is the emotion she has most strongly expressed, she is using outrage as her cool instrument. She uses it with precision to show what monstrosities of feeling come about not from the lack of the existence of love but from love's repudiation, betrayal. From which there is no safety anywhere. Granny Weatherall, eighty, wise, affectionate and good, and now after a full life dying in her bed with the priest beside her, "knew hell when she saw it."

The anger that speaks everywhere in the stories would trouble the heart for their author whom we love except that her anger is pure, the reason for it evident and clear, and the effect exhilarating. She has made it the tool of her work; what we do is rejoice in it. We are aware of the compassion that guides it, as well. Only compassion could have looked where she looks, could have seen and probed what she sees. Real compassion is perhaps always in the end unsparing; it must make itself a part of knowing. Self-pity does not exist here; these stories come out trenchant, bold, defying; they are tough as sanity, unrelinquished sanity, is tough.

Despair is here, as well described as if it were Mexico. It is a despair, however, that is robust and sane, open to negotiation by the light of day. Life seen as a savage ordeal has been investigated by a straightforward courage, unshaken nerve, a rescuing wit, and above all with the searching intelligence that is quite plainly not to be daunted. In the end the stories move us not to despair ourselves but to an emotion quite opposite because they are so seriously and clear-sightedly pointing out what they have been formed to show: that which is true under the skin, that which will remain a fact of the spirit.

Miranda, by the end of "Old Mortality" rebelling against the ties of the blood, resenting their very existence, planning to run away now from these and as soon as she can from her own escape into marriage, Miranda saying "I hate loving and being loved," is hating what destroys loving and what prevents being loved. She is, in her own particular and her own right, fighting back at the cheat she has discovered in all that's been handed down to her as gospel truth.

Seeing what is not there, putting trust in a false picture of life, has been one of the worst nightmares that assail her characters. "My dreams never renege on me, Mr. Richards. They're all I have to go by," says Rosaleen. (The Irish are no better than the Southerners in this respect.) Not only in the comic and touching Rosaleen, the lovely and sentient and tragic Miranda, but in many other characters throughout the stories we watch the romantic and the anti-romantic pulling each other to pieces. Is the romantic ever scotched? I believe not. Even if there rises a new refrain, even if the most ecstatic words ever spoken turn out to be "I hate you," the battle is not over for good. That battle is in itself a romance.

Nothing is so naturally subject to false interpretation as the romantic, and in furnishing that interpretation the Old South can beat all the rest. Yet some romantic things happen also to be true. Miss Porter's stories are not so much a stand against the romantic as such, as a repudiation of the false. What alone can instruct the heart is the experience of living, experience which can be vile; but what can never do it any good, what harms it more than vileness, are those tales, those legends of more than any South, those universal false dreams, the hopes sentimental and ubiquitous, which are not on any account to be gone by.

For there comes a confrontation. It is then that Miss Porter's characters, behaving so entirely like ourselves, make the fatally wrong choice. Enter betrayal. Again and again, enter betrayal. We meet the betrayal that lies in rejection, in saying No to others or No to the self, or that lies with still more cunning in saying Yes when this time it should have been No.

And though we are all but sure what will happen, we are possessed by suspense.

It appears to me irrelevant whether or not the story is conceived and put down in sensory images, whether or not it is dramatic in construction, so long as its hold is a death-grip. In my own belief, the suspense—so acute and so real—in Katherine Anne Porter's work never did depend for its life on disclosure of the happenings of the narrative (nothing is going to turn out very well) but in the writing of the story, which becomes one single long sustained moment for the reader. Its suspense is one with its meaning. It must arise, then, from the mind, heart, spirit by which it moves and breathes.

It is a current like a strand of quicksilver through the serenity of her prose. In fiction of any substance, serenity can only be an achievement of the work itself, for any sentence that is alive with meaning is speaking out of passion. Serenity never belonged to the *now* of writing; it belongs to the later *now* offered its readers. In Katherine Anne Porter's work the forces of passion and self-possession seem equal, holding each other in balance from one moment to the next. The suspense born of the writing abides there in its own character, using the story for its realm, a quiet and well-commanded suspense, but a genie.

There was an instinct I had, trustworthy or not, that the matter of visibility in her stories had something to do with time. Time permeates them. It is a grave and formidable force.

Ask what time it is in her stories and you are certain to get the answer: the hour is fateful. It is not necessary to see the hands of the clock in her work. It is a time of racing urgency, and it is already too late. And then recall how many of her characters are surviving today only for the sake of tomorrow, are living on tomorrow's coming; think how we see them clearest in reference to tomorrow. Granny Weatherall, up to the last—when God gives her no sign acceptable to her and jilts her Himself—is thinking: "There was always so much to be done, let me see: tomorrow." Laura in "Flowering Judas" is "waiting for tomorrow with a bitter anxiety as if tomorrow may not come." Ordinary, self-respecting, and—up to a certain August day—fairly well blessed Mr. Thompson, because he has been the one to kill the abominable Mr. Hatch, is self-tried, self-pleaded for, and self-condemned to no tomorrow; neither does he leave his sons much of a tomorrow, and certainly he leaves still less of one to poor, red-eyed Mrs. Thompson, who had "so wanted to believe that tomorrow, or at least the day after, life, such a battle at best, was going to be better." In "Old Mortality" time takes Miranda by the hand and leads her into promising herself "in her hopefulness, her ignorance": "At least I can know the truth about what happens to me." In "Pale Horse, Pale Rider" the older Miranda asks Adam, out of her suffering, "Why can we not save each other?" and the straight answer is that there is no time. The story ends with the unforgettable words "Now there would be time for everything" because tomorrow has turned into oblivion, the ultimate betrayer is death itself.

But time, one of the main actors in her stories—teacher, fake healer, conspirator in betrayal, ally of death—is also, within the complete control of Miss Porter, with his inimical powers made use of, one of the movers of her writing, a friend to her work. It occurred to me that what is *seeing* the story is the dispassionate eye of time. Her passionate mind has asked itself, schooled itself, to use Time's eye. Perhaps Time is the genie's name.

Laura is stuck in time, we are told in "Flowering Judas"—and told in the timeless present tense of dreaming, a brilliant working upon our very nerves to let us know precisely Laura's dilemma. There is in all Katherine Anne Porter's work the strongest sense of unity in all the parts; and if it is in any degree a sound guess that an important dramatic element in the story has another role, a working role, in the writing of the story, might this not be one source of a unity so deeply felt? Such a thing in the practice of an art is unsurprising. Who can separate a story from the story's writing?

And there is too, in all the stories, a sense of long, learning life, the life that is the story's own, beginning from a long way back, extending somewhere into the future. As we read, the initial spark is not being struck before our eyes; the fire we see has already purified its nature and burns steadied by purpose, unwavering in meaning. It is no longer impulse, it is a signal, a beacon.

To me, it is the image of the eye of time that remains the longest in the mind at her story's end. There is a judgment to be passed. A moral judgment has to be, in all reason, what she has been getting at. But in a still further act of judiciousness, I feel, she lets Time pass that judgment.

Above all, I feel that what we are responding to in Katherine Anne Porter's work is the intensity of its life, which is more powerful and more profound than even its cry for justice.

They are excoriating stories. Does she have any hope for us at all? Well, do we not feel its implication everywhere—a desperate hope for the understanding that may come, if we use great effort, out of tomorrow, or if not then, maybe the day after? Clearly it has to become at some point an act of faith. It is toward this that her stories all point: here, it seems to me, is the North Star.

And how calm is the surface, the invisible surface of it all! In a style as invisible as the rhythm of a voice, and as much her own as her own voice, she tells her stories of horror and humiliation and in the doing fills her readers with a rising joy. The exemplary prose that is without waste or extravagance or self-indulgence or display, without any claim for its triumph, is full of pride. And her reader shares in that pride, as well he might: it is pride in the language, pride in using the language to search out human meanings, pride in the making of a good piece of work. A personal spell is about the stories, the something of her own that we refer to most often, perhaps, when we mention its beauty, and I think this comes from the *making* of the stories.

Readers have long been in the habit of praising (or could it be at times reproaching?) Katherine Anne Porter by calling her a perfectionist. I do not agree that this is the highest praise, and I would think the word misleading, suggesting as it does in the author a personal vanity in technique and a rigidity, even a deadness, in her prose. To me she is something more serious than a perfectionist. I celebrate her for being a blessed achiever. First she is an artist, of course, and as an artist she is an achiever.

That she hasn't wasted precious time repeating herself in her stories is sign enough, if it were needed, that she was never interested in doing the things she knew already that she was able to bring off, that she hasn't been showing off for the sake of high marks (from whom?), but has patiently done what was to her her born necessity, quietly and in her own time, and each time the way she saw fit.

We are left with a sense of statement. Virginia Woolf set down in her diary, on the day when she felt she had seen that great brave difficult novel *The Waves* past a certain point in the writing: "But I think it possible that I have got my statues against the sky." It is the achieving of this crucial, this monumental moment in the work itself that we feel has mattered to Katherine Anne Porter. The reader who looks for the flawless result can find it, but looking for that alone he misses the true excitement, exhilaration, of reading, of re-reading. It is the achieving—in a constant present tense—of the work that shines in the mind when we think of her name; and in that achieving lies, it seems to me, the radiance of the work and our recognition of it as unmistakably her own.

And unmistakable is its source. Katherine Anne Porter's deep sense of fairness and justice, her ardent conviction that we need to give and to receive in loving kindness all the human warmth we can make—here is where her stories come from. If they are made by the mind and address the mind, they draw their eloquence from a passionate heart. And for all their pain, they draw their wit, do they not, from a reserve of natural gayety? I have wondered before now if it isn't those who were born gay who can devote themselves most wholeheartedly in their work to seriousness, who have seriousness to burn. The gay are the rich in feeling, and don't need to save any of it back.

Unmistakable, too, is what this artist has made. Order and form no more spring out of order and form than they come riding in to us upon seashells through the spray. In fiction they have to be made out of their very antithesis, life. The art of making is the thing that has meaning, and I think beauty is likely to be something that has for a time lain under good, patient hands. Whether the finished work of art was easy or hard to make, whether it demanded a few hours or many years, concerns nobody but the maker, but the making itself has shaped that work for good and all. In Katherine Anne Porter's stories we feel their making as a bestowal of grace.

It is out of the response of her particular order and form that I believe I may have learned the simplest and surest reason for why I cannot see her stories in their every passing minute, and why it was never necessary or intended that a reader should. Katherine Anne Porter is writing stories of the spirit, and the time that fills those moments is eternity.

The World of Love:
The Fiction of Eudora Welty

by A lun R. Jones

There has been no doubt of Eudora Welty's standing as a writer since her first collection of stories, *A Curtain of Green,* was published in 1941. Since that time she has consolidated her reputation and confirmed the uniqueness of her achievement by writing two further collections of short stories, *The Wide Net* (1943) and *The Bride of the Innisfallen* (1955), and four longer works of fiction, *The Robber Bridegroom* (1942), *Delta Wedding* (1946), *The Golden Apples* (1949) and *The Ponder Heart* (1956).

Inevitably she has become associated with William Faulkner, Robert Penn Warren, John Crowe Ransom, Allen Tate and that distinguished company of writers who, like Katherine Anne Porter, "have blood knowledge of what life can be in a defeated country on the bare bones of privation." Although she claims Yankee blood on her father's side, she was born in Jackson, Mississippi, not far from the borders of Yoknapatawphaw County, and belongs there in the way that Emily Brontë belongs to the Yorkshire moors. Her close association with the South as a traditional way of life, under pressure and, perhaps, in decay, has been felt to confer on her as a writer special advantages and peculiar limitations, as if she were both the beneficiary and the victim of her background. No one, and certainly not Miss Welty herself, would wish to deny the importance of "place" to a writer, although it could be argued that it is the writers of the South who have made it a place, rather than a point on the compass, just as frontier legend made the West.

Naturally, in her work Miss Welty draws for her material largely on the world of the South, familiar and immediately to hand,
but it is human nature and the human dilemma that are explored,
and her art is distinctive. Only the most provincial reader con-
fuses the writer with the raw material of his art. Certainly the
South seems to lend her an assured sense of personal identity—
because you know where you are, you know who you are—and
this assurance has, in a sense, enabled her to pursue her art with
a freedom and single-mindedness rare among those writers with
apparently more fluid, less stable social backgrounds. But indeed,
even among the writers of the South, she is the only one to have
acknowledged the autonomy of the imagination. Behind her work
there lies a fragile, profound and essentially lyrical imagination
strengthened by characteristic wit and shrewdness. Thus her art
brings together the delicate, introspective refinement of Chekhov,
Katherine Mansfield, and Virginia Woolf and the tough, American know-how of Mark Twain, Stephen Crane and Ring Lardner.

The sheer variety of *A Curtain of Green* is immediately impressive. The stories vary in tone from broad and sometimes grotesque farce to delicate melancholy; there are stories of fairy-tale
simplicity and fantasies of nightmare complexity, stories of
greed, and pride, and horror, and of innocence and love. Yet
above all else they portray a wide variety of attitudes and peoples
living in a recognizably human world of beauty and corruption,
tenderness and hate, wonder and boredom. The stories are concerned largely with single moments of personal crisis and move
towards and explore the nature of conflict as the characters struggle to clarify their choices, to come to terms with themselves and
the world around them. Although a strong sense of an ordered
community binds the settings of the stories together, it is the dark,
inner lives of the characters that interest her more than their
public faces. She is more concerned with individual self-decep-
tion than with social hypocrisy.

She has, too, the storyteller's gift of compelling attention, of
capturing her reader's interest in what happens and, more particularly, in what happens next. Moreover, although her subject
is often fabulous, bizarre and in itself improbable, she has the
unfailing ability to maintain what she has called "believability"
—to establish that imaginative confidence between reader and
writer which constitutes a mutual act of poetic faith.

Stories such as "Death of a Traveling Salesman" and "The Hitchhikers" contrast the settled life of traditional values and the restless commercial world, a contrast between love and loneliness. In "Death of a Traveling Salesman," R. J. Bowman, forced by illness to recognize the restlessness and futility of his life is brought by accident into contact with a couple whose life is slow, intimate and secure. It is the meeting of two worlds, the past and the present, the simple and the complex, the loved and the loveless. Bowman is overwhelmed by the realization of his own emptiness and horrified by his utter inability to communicate at a profound and simple level:

> But he wanted to leap up, to say to her, I have been sick and I found out then, only then, how lonely I am. Is it too late? My heart puts up a struggle inside me, and you may have heard it, protesting against emptiness... It should be full, he would rush on to tell her, thinking of his heart now as a deep lake, it should be holding love like other hearts. It should be flooded with love...

The couple receive Bowman with kindness, hospitality and warmth and without ceremony. He knows he has nothing to offer in return, except money, and in desperation he tries to escape back to the emptiness of his life. His need for love—the struggle his heart puts up inside him—betrays him:

> Just as he reached the road, where his car seemed to sit in the moonlight like a boat, his heart began to give off tremendous explosions like a rifle, bang, bang, bang.
> He sank in fright on to the road, his bags falling about him. He felt as if all this had happened before. He covered his heart with both hands to keep anyone from hearing the noise it made.
> But nobody heard it.

The symbolism in this story (the first to be published) is more direct than in her later stories, but it states the theme that is in so many ways fundamental to an understanding of her fiction: man's loneliness and his search for a world of love.

"The Hitchhikers," for instance, is a more complex and more oblique treatment of a similar theme. A commercial traveler and the two hitchhikers to whom he gives a lift form a community of drifters. Because they exist on the surface of life they are trivial and superficial, unable to give or receive love, unable to realize themselves except as travelers to whom movement from one town to another has become an escape from life. The gratuitousness with which one hitchhiker kills the other, brings home to the commercial traveler an awareness of the rootlessness of his own life. The commercial traveler's ambition is to be "somewhere on a good gravelled road, driving his car past things that happened to people, quicker than their happening." He wants life to be ordered and straightforward and without ties, but life, Miss Welty insists, is a matter of strong roots and slow growth.

Miss Welty reserves her deepest compassion for those who recognize their need for love but are refused—as in the pathetic story of Clytie in *A Curtain of Green,* trapped in a house of lonely and demanding selfishness, who finds release from the sufferings of her absurd, unlovely and unloved life in the companionship of death. Clytie lives in a mysterious world of her own. Aware of the potentiality of wonder and beauty in the world around her, she meets at every turn only horror and brutality. Her spirit is wild and demented with half-understood longings. She is the pathetic victim of her family's selfishness, of a bullying sister, her drunken brother and invalid father. The house is a prison in which the family has interned itself so as to prevent any contact between the Farr family and the villagers of Farr's Gin. Only Clytie goes out, pathetically wandering in the rain and searching for a world of love which she associates faintly with her youth. Later, when the barber is summoned from the village to attend her father, she reaches out "with breath-taking gentleness" towards him only to be rejected in fear. Automatically she obeys her sister's command:

> "Clytie! Clytie! The water! The water!" came Octavia's monumental voice.
>
> Clytie did the only thing she could think of to do. She bent her angular body further, and thrust her head into the barrel, under the water, through its glittering surface into the kind, featureless depth, and held it there.
>
> When Old Lethy found her, she had fallen forward into the barrel, with her poor ladylike black-stockinged legs upended and hung apart like a pair of tongs.

Clytie, a curious kind of Narcissus, has been horrified by the reflection of her own ugly, suffering face. She is shocked into an awareness of how life has perverted and deformed her vision.

She is found, significantly, by her father's devoted nurse whom her sister would not allow into the house. Old Lethy represents childhood and affection trying to re-enter the family but her name suggests death and oblivion. (Frequently in her stories Miss Welty uses classical references. In this particular story the sister is called Octavia, which suggests the cold, Roman matron; and the barber is seen, for a moment, standing "like the statue of Hermes," which wonderfully conveys both his physical attitude and the fact that Clytie mistakenly took him to be a messenger from the better world outside.)

Miss Welty moves with assurance through those worlds of feeling where comedy and pathos meet and become inseparable. "Clytie" is both grimly comic and profoundly moving. There is in the character of Clytie herself a tragic incongruity between the wonder of what we know to be her inner life and the pathetic figure she cuts in her public actions. In the final line when she describes Clytie's legs upended, she shocks us into an awareness of the casual way that life has picked up Miss Clytie and put her down again as if she were quite trivial and dispensable. By reconciling incongruities in this way, Miss Welty shows how tragic feeling can be expressed in laughter, and laughter in her work is often the release of otherwise unbearable pathos.

The stories are often concerned with those who are in some way deprived and living on the very edge of life but they see deprivation not as a social question but as a human one, a matter not of income and status but of love and loneliness. They cover the social range from faded gentry to sharecroppers and Negroes, yet their concern is always with the human dilemma, with man's failure or success in dealing with his own nature, with the realities of the life within him and the needs of those around him.

Each of the stories in *A Curtain of Green* is very different, yet in all of them incident and speech are observed and reported with dispassionate fidelity and patterned with unobtrusive artistry. In "Lily Daw and the Three Ladies," three old spinsters cluck and fuss over their irresponsible charge, desperately trying to reduce her wayward life to some semblance of ordered dignity. The world of Lily Daw is hugely comic and contrasts violently with that of "The Petrified Man" which is fraught with hypocrisy, petty spite, greed and shallow ambitions. The world of the hairdresser and her client in "The Petrified Man" is exposed relentlessly in the course of two conversations between the women. The story has a biting satiric edge that cuts deeply into the vulgar triviality of commercial, small-town life. It is a world both cheap and sinister, in which human relationships have been grotesquely perverted, a world ruthlessly dominated by women who are themselves dominated by spite, cheap sensation and material possessions. The beauty salon is seen as a cave of primeval tortures producing a succession of Medusa-like creatures who turn their men to stone at a glance. The men are impotent before his monstrous regiment of women. The petrified man of the title is an exhibit at a freak show. The discovery that he is "not really petrified at all," but was, in fact, wanted by the police for raping four women provides the story with its climax and with its central symbol. It is a kind of poetic justice to learn that subjugated man has reasserted himself even if in a violent way against this monstrous regiment. The conversation of the women is recorded with amazing fidelity as relentlessly they expose the shallowness and perversity of their own attitudes. The story, emerging casually out of the conversation, is a shrewd and incisive comment on the social scene and shows a complete mastery of the comedy of manners.

"Why I Live at the P.O." is the indignant and gushing monologue—Katherine Anne Porter describes it as a "terrifying case of dementia praecox"—in which the heroine describes how her sister, separated from her husband, comes back home and turns the family against her, forcing her out of the house. The sheer technical skill involved would seem to mark each of these stories as a tour de force, and yet more significant than this is the way in which each, while maintaining a convincing illusion of reality, creates its own world, with its own distinct logic, language and being. Each creates an immediate sense of actuality, of people talking and things happening before the reader's eyes, and this powerful, almost tactual illusion of reality is strongest when the stories themselves are closest to pure fantasy.

Indeed, one of Miss Welty's outstanding characteristics as a writer is her Tennysonian ability to sustain an atmospheric mood. The world of the imagination is so fully realized in terms of the sensuous and ordinary that it is accepted without question. Although these stories are clearly informed by compassionate intelligence and shaped by an acute feeling for artistic form, we are aware that for the author life continually moves towards the fabulous, sometimes—as in "The Petrified Man"—towards the perverse, just as magic shades off into witchcraft. She is conscious of mythical and imaginative reality impinging on and informing the trivial and the banal.

As her stories become longer, her texture richer and more complex in effect, she increasingly explores in depth the world in which the significant and the mythical lie thinly disguised beneath the everyday world around us. In her next collection, *The Wide Net,* she begins to build with gathering assurance on the territory already cleared and charted in her early stories. For, like all great writers, she is continually in competition with herself. In a story such as "First Love" the myth is embodied in the past and is associated particularly with the way in which the past impresses itself on and enriches the present. There is a strong feeling of the organic unity of life, of tradition as a creative, positive force shaping the present and lending individual lives a general validity.

Her imagination is essentially poetic; her fiction is clearly centripetal, structured like poetry with an intuited center and everything subdued to the demands of this central insight. As her art develops, so her fiction accumulates a more profound sense of human suffering and dignity and it covers a wider area of human activity without losing any of its original power. She continues to affirm the beauties and terrors inherent in the human situation while asserting the right to love and the need to dream. Through dream, as through art, man can express and realize his secret self: through love, as through art, he can communicate that secret self to others; for art, she believes, is the power to convey love. In "A Still Moment" she brings together the themes of loneliness, love and time, "God's giving Separateness first and then giving Love to follow and heal in its wonder." The tragedy of man is to be separate and lonely, his glory is to be capable of dissolving his loneliness in love.

Legend, a more specific land of mythology, plays a larger part in her later work. In "First Love" and in "A Still Moment" she incorporates legendary figures into the story. "First Love," for instance, is concerned with Joel Mayes, a deaf and dumb boy who is caught up in the romantic and mysterious conspiracy of Aaron Burr. Painfully, through love, the boy achieves self-awareness.

The love is, of necessity, unspoken and unacknowledged. His life is touched by the historical past being enacted around him and he achieves self-consciousness, shame, love and adulthood. The unthinking innocence of childhood is lost to him and his life to that point takes on an entirely different meaning. Even the world of nature, to which he was formerly drawn as by a bond of sympathy, now seems completely changed:

> He held the bud, and studied the burned edges of its folds by the pale half-light of the East. The buds came apart in his hand, its layers like small velvet shells, still iridescent, the shrivelled flower inside. He held it tenderly and yet timidly, in a kind of shame, as though all disaster lay pitifully disclosed now to the eyes.

In a way the story re-enacts the Fall of Man, the child moving out of the world of innocence into the world of experience. It is the kind of romantic dynamic associated with Blake who also regarded love as the great regenerative force by virtue of which man could regain a vision of that Eden from which self-conscious knowledge had exiled him. There is a general feeling in Miss Welty's work that man, driven forward by dreams of the future has, with dignity and humor, created a precarious present out of the wilderness and chaos of the past.

Her novel *The Robber Bridegroom* is a direct tribute to the legendary past. Set in Mississippi in 1798 when it was still Spanish, the action is mostly centered on the Old Natchez Trace which ran for two hundred miles through the wilderness between Natchez and Nashville. The story opens in Rodney's Landing— now a ghost town—with a mock-heroic encounter between the two legendary figures, Mike Fink and Jamie Lockhart, and ends in New Orleans with the happy reunion of Jamie Lockhart, the Robber Bridegroom, and Rosamond, his bride. In this brilliant, loving parody of fairy tale, the legends of the past are recreated with magical simplicity and directness. All the elements of the fairy tale, including its traditional style, are accommodated; the heroes are suitably romantic and heroic; the heroine is virtuous and trusting, with a proper sense of curiosity; the wicked step-mother is, of course, in league with the forces of evil and plotting against the heroine; the father is kind and doting and everyone— at least every one of the virtuous characters—lives happily ever after. Miss Welty's attitude towards her material is detached, even ironic, though she leaves no doubt that it is a parody written without sentimentality but with profound admiration and respect.

In *Delta Wedding*, her second novel, she returns to a study of childhood innocence in contact and often in conflict with the authoritarian world of adult experience. The story is of a nine-year-old girl's visit to the Fairchilds', her introduction to the lives of her cousins and their complex world of aunts and friends. But the novel is much more than the story of a young girl's seven-day stay with relatives, for the journey from Jackson to the Fairchilds' is a journey into the new and frightening world of experience. Delicately, the novel probes expanding possibilities, excitements and responsibilities and with precision of feeling defines the child's vivid responses to the world around her.

Written in a style in which poetry and prose blend, mood and landscape knit in a meaningful whole, so that the reader is able to enter unobtrusively into the private thoughts, discontents and happiness of the characters. The family is dominated by Uncle George and the theme of love is embodied in him. The life of the Fairchilds is ordered, possessive and resentful of outsiders. Uncle George is portrayed as a man of selfless courage and "wild detachment," who is guided not by the social patterns of behavior which the others expect and understand but by some older tradition of personal integrity. The family possessively makes demands on him and cannot forgive him because he "loved the *world. ...* Not them in particular"; and indeed one of the main themes of the novel is the struggle of his wife to accept the disinterested quality of her husband's love which she felt by rights ought to belong to her alone.

Miss Welty continually stresses the universality of this love which belongs to no one but is available to everyone. Ellen—mother, wife and sister—who is the novel's central character comes to recognize, accept and value the quality of George's love and to see that whatever life and fate handed out to him ("Ready for anything all the time") he would always meet it with that same disinterested passion. The social life at "Shellmound" follows an accepted, almost ritualistic pattern, social relationships are clearly defined; Dabney is marrying "beneath" her in marrying Troy, an overseer, as indeed Uncle George has already shocked the family by marrying Robbie, who worked in the local store.

Uncle George defines to a large extent Miss Welty's conception of the world of love, although as a character he is always in the end remote, mysterious and even mythological. Nevertheless, the central impulse in *Delta Wedding* does not seem strong enough to hold a novel together. The reader is aware of the danger that the novel might fall into sections and episodes which are not strongly interdependent.

Perhaps it was to avoid this tendency that Miss Welty wrote her next book, *The Golden Apples*, in sections rather than in the form of a traditional novel. Undoubtedly the seven separate stories create a unity of a sort, linked as they are by their locale, a small town, Morgana, and by the reappearance of many of the same characters throughout. The stories vary in tone from the broad comedy of "Shower of Gold" to the desperate melancholy of "The Whole World Knows." "Shower of Gold" tells of the disappearance and reappearance of Snowdie MacLain's husband. Like so many of her stories, this one is characterized by a strong feeling for the casual—the mark of the consummate craftsman. The more extraordinary the event, the more the style tends toward the throw-away. The opening of "Shower of Gold" is a fine example:

> That was Miss Snowdie MacLain.
> She comes after her butter, won't let me run over with it from just across the road. Her husband walked out of the house one day and left his hat on the banks of the Big Black River.—That could have started something, too.
> We might have had a little run on doing that in Morgana, if it had been so willed. What King did, the copy-cats always might do. Well, King MacLain left a new straw hat on the banks of the Big Black and there are people that consider he headed West.

Her use of the garrulous narrator not only enables her to exploit her uncanny gift for reproducing the authentic accents of colloquial speech but provides her with another source of interest in the character of the narrator as well as another perspective.

In "June Recital," the most complex of these stories, she uses two quite different narrators to define two quite separate attitudes toward the same incident. The young boy, Loch, and his older sister, Cassie, are both spectators of the sinister happening in the deserted house next door. Loch sees a sailor making love to a girl

in an upstairs room and an old woman scattering paper around
the living room downstairs who then sits down to play the piano.
Loch in his innocence accepts these events with wonder but without serious questioning; Cassie, a little more experienced than
her brother, questions these events and tries to make sense of
them, but her mind is on the hayride for which she is making herself ready. Thus three lives and three points of view are brought
together, each working at a different level of consciousness, but
each in its separate way affected by the others. One is without
experience or anticipation, one with a little experience is filling
her life with the excitement of anticipation, the third, old, deranged and embittered, has had her ambitions and expectations
cruelly frustrated. Yet the story as a whole affirms the mystery
and wonder of life rather than its disappointments.

Similarly, in "The Whole World Knows," which tells the story
of Randall MacLain's desertion by Jinny Love and his affair
with Maideen Sumrall, the tone is pervasively melancholic, but
it is life itself that is affirmed—in spite of the treachery of time
and transience. Indeed, the town of Morgana suggests the
claustrophobic, painful and distracting landscape in which all
of us, in a sense, came to terms with the adult world for the first
time. It is a different place for each character as they emerge
from their private worlds to face the larger world outside. It is
essentially a secure landscape, still to some extent dominated by
parents.

What the characters in *The Golden Apples* all learn is that to
live in harmony demands a strenuous act of creation; it entails
reshaping one's inner world to meet the needs of others. In fact,
The Golden Apples maps that whole area of consciousness that we
vaguely call "growing up." It is in many ways Miss Welty's most
complex and satisfying achievement, for she seems to be drawing
on all her considerable resources, both technical and thematic,
and bringing them together to make a statement about life that is
rich and profound in all its fabulous, banal, comic, tragic and
human variety.

Morgana becomes finally as complete a map of Eudora Welty's
imaginative world as she has given us. The act of creative imagination is seen now to be the act of life itself. The effort of living is
an act of imagination, and like the regeneration of the Ancient
Mariner (which has often been interpreted as a poem about the

workings of the creative imagination) must begin with an act of love.

Allen Tate once observed that "the typical Southern conversation is not going anywhere, it is not about anything. It is about the people who are talking—conversation is only an expression of manners, the purpose of which is to make everybody happy." Miss Welty's hugely comic book, *The Ponder Heart,* is clearly written in this tradition. Breathlessly, Edna Earle describes the life of her Uncle Daniel—a life devoted to making everybody happy. Uncle Daniel is the richest man in the small town of Clay although money means nothing to him, for the world in which he lives is the golden world of the heart where wealth is counted in love, generosity, kindness and happiness. As Edna says, "If he ever did a thing to be sorry for, it's more than he ever intended." Uncle Daniel lives in the world he has created for himself, a beautiful, absurd world of love. According to his niece, his great weaknesses are that he loves people and loves giving things away:

> Things I could think of without being asked that he's given away
> would be—a string of hams, a fine suit of clothes, a white-face heifer
> calf, two trips to Memphis, a pair of fantail pigeons, fine Shetland
> pony (loves children), brooder and incubator, good nanny goat,
> bad billy, cypress cistern, field of white Dutch clover, two iron
> wheels and some laying pullets (they were together), cow pasture
> during drought (he has everlasting springs), innumerable fresh
> eggs, a pick-up truck—even his own cemetery lot, but they wouldn't
> accept it...

Uncle Daniel's generosity is indiscriminate—the incubator he gave to the postman, not that he "ever got a *letter* in his life." Even the Beulah Hotel that Edna Earle owns was given to her by Uncle Daniel. For the most part the town regards him as simple-minded—his father considered him positively unbalanced and had him put in an asylum—though because some of the magic of his life has rubbed off on them, they also regard him with admiration. Edna Earle is mainly concerned with her uncle's relationship with Bonnie Dee Peacock, her death and Uncle Daniel's trial for her murder. Uncle Daniel found Bonnie Dee working in a ten-cent store and persuaded her to agree to a marriage trial. The marriage trial went on for five years and six

months before "Bonnie Dee, if you please, decided No." When
Bonnie Dee leaves him she is persuaded to return by an advertisement placed by Edna in the Memphis *Commercial Appeal*. The
advertisement, in the form of a poem entitled "Come Back to
Clay," was successful. The first thing she does when she comes
back is to force Uncle Daniel to leave. Uncle Daniel moves into
the Beulah Hotel but is happy, for, as he explains, "Oh, my bride
has come back to me. Pretty as a picture, and I'm happy beyond
compare." While to everybody else Bonnie Dee is an empty-
headed, stupid, young girl, she remains beautiful in Uncle
Daniel's eyes.

Bonnie Dee is incapable of love, though Uncle Daniel has
more than enough for two, and, when she is finally bribed to
accept him back in the house, he finds her crying with fright at
the thunderstorm outside. In order to distract her, Uncle Daniel
begins to tickle her and she dies—laughing. At the trial, Uncle
Daniel's world of love is exposed to the hard light of logic and
reason by Mr. Gladney, the prosecuting lawyer, but it is Uncle
Daniel's world that prevails and the world of Mr. Gladney that
crumbles away into senseless greed. Uncle Daniel is impregnable
and incorruptible for, as Edna Earle explains, "he's been brought
up in a world of love." *The Ponder Heart* is a glorious comic
invention, a masterpiece of contrived lunacy that affirms love as
the source of human activity and Uncle Daniel a fabulous representative of human virtue.

In her latest collection of stories, *The Bride of the Innisfallen,*
Miss Welty has broadened the scope, as well as enriched the texture of her writing still further. Her eye and her ear are as sharp
as ever, but her compassion leads her to a more subdued consideration of personal suffering. Her work takes on a sculptured,
timeless solidity. At the same time, her thematic material becomes denser and more complex, and an increased artistic assurance enables her to treat her narrative more obliquely than in
her previous work. She no longer draws her material exclusively
from the South and she explores new areas of experience with
more somber restraint and from a viewpoint withdrawn from the
center of the stories' interest. Taken as a whole the stories are
an exciting departure. They are experiments in a kind of impres-
sionistic writing that depends hardly at all on traditional narra-

tive techniques but relies largely on *montage*, an approach to writing that has its parallel in the cinema of the *Nouvelle Vague*. Three of the stories in this volume—"No Place for You, My Love," "The Bride of the Innisfallen," and "Going to Naples"—are concerned with journeys and with strangers briefly and loosely thrown together because of their common destination. The climax of each story is arrived at obliquely as imperceptibly the consciousness of each character leaves its impression on his fellow travelers.

For example, "No Place for You, My Love" is deliberately vague on the conventional level of plot and characterization. A man and a woman, not themselves southerners, meet accidentally in a New Orleans restaurant and take a car ride over the Mississippi toward the South. They drive compulsively onwards through the intense and merciless heat into a country which becomes more unreal the further they travel. They are exposed finally to a wasteland of light without shadows and without purpose—except that they follow the road, until the road just ends. The journey has many of the features of a bad dream as the couple unknown to each other move deeper and deeper into a country which is also unknown. There is little conversation between them and everything that happens appears, as in a nightmare, to be both significant and inconsequential. At the nadir of their journey, which is also the turning point, they dance together in a strange bar. They dance formally, "like professional, Spanish dancers wearing masks," and the dance establishes the relationship between them. This relationship, tenuous, formal, with a quiet undertow of passion, haunts them on their return journey back to normality. It is as if they had visited the underworld together so that when they step back into their old lives and the familiar world, this ghostly relationship "cried like a human, and dropped back."

The story is completely unified at a symbolic, impressionist level and the mood is sustained with great subtlety. Although at the end of the story we know little more about the characters than we did at the beginning, there is a sense also in which we know all there is to know about them. The story is a complete and satisfying "objective correlative" for a certain kind of shock experienced by those with courage enough to face life unprotected by the buffers of habit or custom. Similarly, "The Burning"

is a pitiless exposure of a deranged world set at the time of the
Civil War when Sherman was marching and burning his way
through the South. The tone of these stories is meditative and
compassionate and depicts a strange modern Odyssey into disturbing areas of human consciousness.

Each of Miss Welty's works seems to present her with a different
challenge and in each she has extended herself in a new direction.
For her, writing is a means of exploration and in the stories of
The Bride of the Innisfallen she reaches deep into a new and
darker side of experience.

Miss Welty has stated her belief that:

> ...each novel written stands as something of a feat. For what has
> been done? First ask, what was the heart's desire? Not the creating
> of an illusion, but the restoring of one; something brought off. We
> are not children once we have pasts; and now as we come looking in
> fiction with more longing than in any experience save love, but to
> which love adds, looking for reflections and visions of all life we
> know compounded through art, performance itself is what we ask
> for. We ask only that it be magic. Good fiction grants this boon, bad
> denies it. And performance is what the novelists would like to give
> ...a fresh performance; not to show off skill, which would be...a
> thing to be despised, but, out of respect, love, and fearlessness for
> all that may be tried, to command the best skill.

Between *A Curtain of Green* and *The Bride of the Innisfallen*
Miss Welty has developed a vision of life that is matched by her
consummate skill. Writing with love, she restores our illusions
about the world of love. Her fiction is exuberant with life, rich in
comedy, pathos and color, quick with movement and firmly disci-
plined. Each of her stories creates its own level of reality and
succeeds in the business of fiction which is to make reality real.
Replete with sensuous and meaningful detail, the meaning itself
is often suspended in that private world somewhere between
dreaming and waking. Indeed, it is the particular, personal
moment that her imagination seizes with concrete and urgent
immediacy.

Her writing as a whole is characterized by an elegant and correct compassion that interpenetrates life's disordered vitality in
such a way that, in her own words, "life on earth is intensified in
its personal meaning and so restored to human terms." Her art
shapes the experience, lending it style and direction; life informs

her art at every turn, giving it variety and intensity. The most immediate and most lasting impression created by reading her work is an admiration for the sheer abundance of human life. Her achievement has won her comparison with the best writers of the century and the prospect of her future work assures readers of fresh and exciting excellence.

Love and Separateness
in Eudora Welty

by Robert Penn Warren

> He could understand God's giving Separateness first and
> then giving Love to follow and heal in its wonder; but
> God had reversed this, and given Love first and then
> Separateness, as though it did not matter to Him which
> came first.—"A Still Moment"

If we put *The Wide Net,* Eudora Welty's second collection of
stories, up against her first collection, *A Curtain of Green,* we can
immediately observe a difference: the stories of *The Wide Net*
represent a specializing, an intensifying, of one of the many
strains which were present in *A Curtain of Green.* All of the
stories in *A Curtain of Green* bear the impress of Miss Welty's
individual talent, but there is a great variety among them in subject matter and method and, more particularly, mood. It is almost
as if the author had gone at each story as a fresh start in the business of writing fiction, as if she had had to take a new angle each
time out of a joy in the pure novelty of the perspective. We find
the vindictive farce of "The Petrified Man," the nightmare of
"Clytie," the fantasy and wit of "Old Mr. Marblehall," the ironic
self-revelation of "Why I Live at the P.O.," the nearly straight
realism of "The Hitch-Hikers," the macabre comedy and pathos
of "Keela, the Outcast Indian Maiden." The material of many of
the stories was sad, or violent, or warped, and even the comedy

and wit were not straight, but if read from one point of view, if read as a performance, the book was exhilarating, even gay, as though the author were innocently delighted not only with the variety of the world but with the variety of ways in which one could look at the world and the variety of things that stories could be and still be stories. Behind the innocent delight of the craftsman, and of the admirer of the world, there was also a seriousness, a philosophical cast of mind, which gave coherence to the book, but on the surface there was the variety, the succession of surprises. In *The Wide Net* we do not find the surprises. The stories are more nearly cut to one pattern.

We do not find the surprises. Instead, on the first page, with the first sentence of the first story, "First Love," we enter a special world: "Whatever happened, it happened in extraordinary times, in a season of dreams..." And that is the world in which we are going to live until we reach the last sentence of the last story. "Whatever happened," the first sentence begins, as though the author cannot be quite sure what did happen, cannot quite undertake to resolve the meaning of the recorded event, cannot, in fact, be too sure of recording all of the event. This is coyness, of course; or a way of warning the reader that he cannot expect quite the ordinary direct light on the event. For it is "a season of dreams"— and the faces and gestures and events often have something of the grave retardation, the gnomic intensity, the portentous suggestiveness of dreams. The logic of things here is not quite the logic by which we live, or think we live, our ordinary daylight lives. In "The Wide Net," for example, the young husband, who thinks his wife has jumped into the river, goes out with a party of friends to dredge for the body, but the sad occasion turns into a saturnalian fish-fry which is interrupted when the great King of the Snakes raises his hoary head from the surface of the river. But usually, in *The Wide Net*, the wrenching of logic is not in terms of events themselves, though "The Purple Hat" is a fantasy, and "Asphodel" moves in the direction of fantasy. Usually the events as events might be given a perfectly realistic treatment Dreiser could take the events of "The Landing" for a story). But in these cases where the events and their ordering are "natural" and not supernatural or fantastic, the stories themselves finally belong to the "season of dreams" because of the special tone and mood, the special perspective, the special sensibility with which they are rendered.

Some readers, in fact, who are quite aware of Miss Welty's gifts, have recently reported that they are disturbed by the recent development of her work. Diana Trilling, in her valuable and sobering comments on current fiction, which appear regularly in the *Nation,* says that the author "has developed her technical virtuosity to the point where it outweighs the uses to which it is put, and her vision of horror to the point of nightmare." There are two ideas in this indictment, and let us take the first one first and come to the second much later. The indictment of the technique is developed along these lines: Miss Welty has made her style too fancy—decorative, "falsely poetic" and "untrue," "insincere." ("When an author says 'look at me' instead of 'look at it,' there is insincerity....") This insincerity springs from "the extreme infusion of subjectivism and private sensibility." But the subjectivism, Mrs. Trilling goes on to say, leads not only to insincerity and fine writing but to a betrayal of the story's obligation to narrative and rationality. Miss Welty's stories take off from a situation, but "the stories themselves stay with their narrative no more than a dance, say, stays with its argument." That is the summary of the indictment.

The indictment is, no doubt, well worth the close attention of Miss Welty's admirers. There is, in fact, a good deal of the falsely poetic in Miss Welty's present style, metaphors that simply pretend to an underlying logic, and metaphors (and descriptions) that, though good themselves, are irrelevant to the business in hand. And sometimes Miss Welty's refusal to play up the objective action—her attempt to define and refine the response rather than to present the stimulus—does result in a blurred effect. But the indictment treats primarily not of such failures to fulfill the object the artist has set herself but of the nature of that object. The critic denies, in effect, that Miss Welty's present kind of fiction is fiction at all: "It is a book of ballets, not of stories."

Now is it possible that the critic is arguing from some abstract definition of "story," some formalistic conception which does not accommodate the present exhibit, and is not concerning herself with the question of whether or not the present exhibit is doing the special job which it proposes for itself, and, finally, the job which we demand of all literature? Perhaps we should look at a

new work first in terms of its effect and not in terms of a definition of type, because every new work is in some degree, however
modest, wrenching our definition, straining its seams, driving
us back from the formalistic definition to the principles on which
the definition was based. Can we say this, therefore, of our ex-
pectation concerning a piece of literature, new or old: That it
should intensify our awareness of the world (and of ourselves in
relation to the world) in terms of an idea, a "view." This leads us
to what is perhaps the key statement by Diana Trilling concerning *The Wide Net:* she grants that the volume "has tremendous
emotional impact, despite its obscurity." In other words, she says,
unless I misinterpret her, that the book does intensify the reader's
awareness—but *not* in terms of a presiding idea.

This has led me to reread Miss Welty's two volumes of stories
in the attempt to discover the issues which are involved in the
"season of dreams." To begin with, almost all of the stories deal
with people who, in one way or another, are cut off, alienated,
isolated from the world. There is the girl in "Why I Live at the
P.O."—isolated from her family by her arrogance, meanness,
and sense of persecution; the half-witted Lily Daw, who, despite
the efforts of "good" ladies, wants to live like other people; the
deaf-mutes of "The Key," and the deaf-mute of "First Love";
the people of "The Whistle" and "A Piece of News," who are
physically isolated from the world and who make their pathetic
efforts to re-establish something lost; the traveling salesman and
the hitch-hikers of "The Hitch-Hikers," who, for their different
reasons, are alone, and the traveling salesman of "Death of a
Traveling Salesman" who, in the physically and socially isolated
backwoods cabin, discovers that he is the one who is truly isolated;
Clytie, isolated in family pride and madness and sexual frustra-
tion, and Jennie of "At the Landing," and Mrs. Larkin of "A Curtain of Green," the old women of "A Visit of Charity" and the old
Negro woman of "A Worn Path"; the murderer of "Flowers for
Marjorie," who is cut off by an economic situation and the pressure of a great city; Mr. Marblehall in his secret life; Livvie, who,
married to an old man and trapped in his respectable house, is
cut off from the life appropriate to her years; Lorenzo, Murrell,
and Audubon in "A Still Moment," each alone in his dream, his
obsession; the old maids of "Asphodel," who tell the story of Miss
Sabina and then are confronted by the naked man and pursued by

the flock of goats. In some of the cases, the matter is more in-
directly presented. For instance, in "Keela, the Outcast Indian
Maiden," we find, as in *The Ancient Mariner*, the story of a man
who, having committed a crime, must try to re-establish his connection with humanity; or in the title story of *The Wide Net*, William Wallace, because he thinks his wife has drowned herself, is
at the start of the story cut off from the world of natural joy in
which he had lived.

We can observe that the nature of the isolation may be different
from case to case, but the fact of isolation, whatever its nature,
provides the basic situation of Miss Welty's fiction. The drama
which develops from this basic situation is of either of two kinds:
first, the attempt of the isolated person to escape into the world;
or second, the discovery by the isolated person, or by the reader,
of the nature of the predicament.

As an example of the first type, we can remember Clytie's obsessed inspection of faces ("Was it possible to comprehend the
eyes and the mouth of other people, which concealed she knew
not what, and secretly asked for still another unknown thing?")
and her attempt to escape, and to solve the mystery, when she lays
her finger on the face of the terrified barber who has come to the
ruinous old house to shave her father. Or there is Jennie, of "At
the Landing," or Livvie, or the man of "Keela." As an example of
the second type, there is the new awareness on the part of the
salesman in "The Hitch-Hikers," or the new awareness on the
part of the other salesman in the back-country cabin.

Even in "A Still Moment" we have this pattern, though in
triplicate. The evangelist Lorenzo, the outlaw Murrell, and the
naturalist and artist Audubon stand for a still moment and watch
a white heron feeding. Lorenzo sees a beauty greater than he can
account for (he had earlier "accounted for" the beauty by thinking, "Praise God, His love has come visible"), and with the swea
of rapture pouring down from his forehead, shouts into the
marshes, "Tempter!" He has not been able to escape from his own
obsession, or in other words, to make his definition of the world
accommodate the white heron and the "natural" rapture which
takes him. Murrell, looking at the bird, sees "only whiteness en
sconced in darkness," and thinks that "if it would look at him
dream penetration would fill and gratify his heart"—the hear
which Audubon has already defined as belonging to the flint

darkness of a cave. Neither Lorenzo nor Murrell can "love" the bird, and so escape from their own curse as did, again, the Ancient Mariner. But there remains the case of Audubon himself, who does "love" the bird, who can innocently accept nature. There is, however, an irony here. To paint the bird he must "know" the bird as well as "love" it, he must know it feather by feather, he must have it in his hand. And so he must kill it. But having killed the bird, he knows that the best he can make of it now in a painting would be a dead thing, "never the essence, only a sum of parts," and that "it would always meet with a stranger's sight, and never be one with beauty in any other man's head in the world." Here, too, the fact of the isolation is realized: as artist and lover of nature he had aspired to a communication, a communion, with other men in terms of the bird, but now "he saw his long labor most revealingly at the point where it met its limit" and he is forced back upon himself.

"A Still Moment," however, may lead us beyond the discussion of the characteristic situation, drama, and realization in Miss Welty's stories. It may lead us to a theme which seems to underlie the stories. For convenience, though at the risk of incompleteness, or even distortion, we may call it Innocence and Experience. Let us take Audubon in relation to the heron. He loves the bird, innocently, in its fullness of being. But he must subject this love to knowledge; he must kill the bird if he is to commemorate its beauty, if he is to establish his communion with the other men in terms of the bird's beauty. There is in the situation an irony of limit and contamination.

Let us look at this theme in relation to other stories. "A Memory," in *A Curtain of Green,* gives a simple example. Here we have a young girl lying on a beach and looking out at the scene through a frame made by her fingers, for the girl can say of herself, "To watch everything about me I regarded grimly and possessively as a need." (As does Audubon, in "A Still Moment.") And further: "It did not matter to me what I looked at; from any observation I would conclude that a secret of life had been nearly revealed to me. ..." Now the girl is cherishing a secret love, a love for a boy at school about whom she knows nothing, to whom she has never even spoken, but whose wrist her hand had once accidentally brushed. The secret love had made her watching of the world more austere, had sharpened her demand that the world conform to her own ideas, and had created a sense of fear. This fear had seemed to be realized one day when, in the middle of a class, the boy had a fit of nosebleed. But that is in the past. This morning she suddenly sees between the frame of her fingers a group of coarse, fat, stupid, and brutal people disporting themselves on the sand with a maniacal, aimless vigor which comes to climax when the fat woman, into the front of whose bathing suit the man had poured sand, bends over and pulls down the cloth so that the lumps of mashed and folded sand empty out. "I felt a peak of horror, as though her breasts themselves had turned to sand, as though they were of no importance at all and she did not care." Over against this defilement (a defilement which implies that the body, the breasts which turn to sand, has no meaning), there is the refuge of the dream, "the undefined austerity of my love."

"A Memory" presents the moment of the discovery of the two poles—the dream and the world; the idea and nature; innocence and experience; individuality and the anonymous, devouring life-flux; meaning and force; love and knowledge. It presents the contrast in terms of horror (as do "The Petrified Man" and "Why I Live at the P.O." when taken in the context of Miss Welty's work) and with the issue left in suspension, but other stories present it with different emphases and tonalities.

For instance, when William Wallace, in "The Wide Net," goes out to dredge the river, he is presumably driven by the fear that his wife has jumped in, but the fear is absorbed into the world of the river, and in a saturnalian revel he prances about with a great catfish hung on his belt, like a river-god laughing and leaping. But he had also dived deep down into the water: "Had he suspected down there, like some secret, the real true trouble that Hazel had fallen into, about which words in a letter could not speak…how (who knew?) she had been filled to the brim with that elation that they all remembered, like their own secret, the elation that comes of great hopes and changes, sometimes simply of the harvest time, that comes with a little course of its own like a tune to run in the head, and there was nothing she could do about it, they knew—and so it had turned into this? It could be nothing but the old trouble that William Wallace was finding out, reaching and turning in the gloom of such depths."

This passage comes clear when we recall that Hazel, the wife who is supposed to have committed suicide by drowning, is pregnant: she had sunk herself in the devouring life-flux, has lost her individuality there, just as the men hunting for the body have lost the meaning of their mission. For the river is simply force, which does not have its own definition; in it are the lost string of beads to wind around the little Negro boy's head, the catfish for the feast, the baby alligator that looks "like the oldest and worst lizard," and the great King of the Snakes. As Doc, the wise old man who owns the net, says: "The outside world is full of endurance." And he also says: "The excursion is the same when you go looking for your sorrow as when you go looking for your joy." Man has the definition, the dream, but when he plunges into the river he runs the risk of having it washed away. But it is important to notice that in this story, there is not horror at the basic contrast, but a kind of gay acceptance of the issue: when William Wallace gets home he finds that his wife had fooled him, and spanks her, and then she lies smiling in the crook of his arm. "It was the same as any other chase in the end."

As "The Wide Net," unlike "A Memory," does more than merely present the terms of contrast, so do such stories as "Livvie" and "At the Landing." Livvie, who lives in the house of wisdom (her infirm husband's name is Solomon) and respectability (the dream, the idea, which has withered) and Time (there is the gift of the silver watch), finally crosses into the other world, the world of the black buck, the field hand, in his Easter clothes—another god, not a river-god but a field god. Just after Solomon's death, the field hand in his gorgeous Easter clothes takes Livvie in his arms, and she drops the watch which Solomon had given her, while outside "the redbirds were flying and crisscrossing, the sun was in all the bottles on the prisoned trees, and the young peach was shining in the middle of them with the bursting light of spring."

If Livvie's crossing into the world of the field god is joyous, the escape of Jennie, in "At the Landing," is rendered in a different tonality. This story assimilates into a new pattern many of the elements found in "A Memory," "The Wide Net," "Livvie," and "Clytie." As in the case of Clytie, Jennie is caught in the house of pride, tradition, history, and as in the case of Livvie, in a house of death. The horror which appears in "A Memory," in "Clytie," reappears here. The basic symbolism of "Livvie" and of "The Wide Net" is again called into play. The river, as in "The Wide Net," is the symbol of that world from which Jennie is cut off. The grandfather's dream at the very beginning sets up the symbolism which is developed in the action:

> "The river has come back. That Floyd came to tell me. The sun was shining full on the face of the church, and that Floyd came around it with his wrist hung with a great long catfish.... That Floyd's catfish has gone loose and free.... And all of a sudden, my dears— my dears, it took its river life back, and shining so brightly swam through the belfry of the church, and downstream."

Floyd, the untamed creature of uncertain origin, is like William Wallace, the river-god dancing with the great catfish at his belt. But he is also, like the buck in "Livvie," a field god, riding the red horse in a pasture full of butterflies. He is free and beautiful, and Jennie is drawn after him, for "she knew that he lived apart in delight." But she also sees him scuffling playfully with the hideous old Mag: the god does not make nice distinctions. When the flood comes over the Landing (upsetting the ordered lives, leaving slime in the houses), Floyd takes her in his boat to a hill (significantly the cemetery hill where her people are buried), violates her, feeds her wild meat and fish (field and river), and when the flood is down, leaves her. She has not been able to talk to him, and when she does say, "I wish you and I could be far away. I wish for a little house," he only stares into the fire as though he hasn't heard a word. But after he has gone she cannot live longer in the Landing; she must find him.

Her quest leads her into the dark woods (which are like an underwater depth) and to the camp of the wild river people, where the men are throwing knives at a tree. She asks for Floyd, but he is not there. The men put her in a grounded houseboat and come in to her. "A rude laugh covered her cry, and somehow both the harsh human sounds could easily have been heard as rejoicing, going out over the river in the dark night." Jennie has crossed into the other world to find violence and contamination, but there is not merely the horror as in "Clytie" and "A Memory." Jennie has acted out a necessary role: she has moved from the house of death, like Livvie, and there is "gain" as well as "loss." We must not forget the old woman who looks into the dark houseboat, a the very end of the story, and understands when she is told that the strange girl is "waiting for Billy Floyd." The old woman nods "out to the flowing river, with the firelight following her face and showing its dignity."

If this general line of interpretation is correct, we find that the stories represent variations on the same basic theme, on the contrasts already enumerated. It is not that there is a standard resolution for the contrasts which is repeated from story to story; rather, the contrasts, being basic, are not susceptible of a single standard resolution, and there is an implicit irony in Miss Welty's work. But if we once realize this, we can recognize that the contrasts are understood not in mechanical but in vital terms: the contrasts provide the terms of human effort, for the dream must be carried to, submitted to, the world, innocence to experience, love to knowledge, knowledge to fact, individuality to communion. What resolution is possible is, if I read the stories with understanding, in terms of the vital effort. The effort is a "mystery," because it is in terms of the effort, doomed to failure but essential, that the human manifests itself as human. Again and again, in different forms, we find what we find in Joel of "First Love": "Joel would never know now the true course, or the true outcome of any dream: this was all he felt. But he walked on, in the frozen path into the wilderness, on and on. He did not see how he could ever go back and still be the boot-boy at the Inn."

It is possible that, in trying to define the basic issue and theme of Miss Welty's stories, I have made them appear too systematic, too mechanical. I do not mean to imply that her stories should be read as allegories, with a neat point-to-point equating of image and idea. It is true that a few of her stories, such as "The Wide Net," do approach the limit of allegory, but even in such cases we find rather than the system of allegory a tissue of symbols which emerge from, and disappear into, a world of scene and action which, once we discount the author's special perspective, is recognizable in realistic terms. The method is similar to the method of much modern poetry, and to that of much modern fiction and drama, but at the same time it is a method as old as fable, myth, and parable. It is a method by which the items of fiction (scene, action, character, etc.) are presented not as document but as comment, not as a report but as a thing made, not as history but as idea. Even in the most realistic and reportorial fiction, the social picture, the psychological analysis, and the pattern of action do not rest at the level of mere report; they finally operate as expressive symbols as well.

Fiction may be said to have two poles, history and idea, and the emphasis may be shifted very far in either direction. In the present collection the emphasis has been shifted very far in the direction of idea, but at the same time there remains a sense of the vividness of the actual world: the picnic of "The Wide Net" is a real picnic as well as a "journey," Cash of "Livvie" is a real field hand in his Easter clothes as well as a field god. In fact, it may be said that when the vividness of the actual world is best maintained, when we get the sense of one picture superimposed upon another, different and yet somehow the same, the stories are most successful.

The stories which fail are stories like "The Purple Hat" and "Asphodel," in which the material seems to be manipulated in terms of an idea, in which the relation between the image and the vision has become mechanical, in which there is a strain, in which we do find the kind of hocus-pocus deplored by Diana Trilling.

And this brings us back to the criticism that the volume "has tremendous emotional impact, despite its obscurity," that the "fear" it engenders is "in inverse ratio to its rational content." Now it seems to me that this description does violence to my own experience of literature, that we do not get any considerable emotional impact unless we sense, at the same time, some principle of organization, some view, some meaning. This does not go to say that we have to give an abstract formulation to that principle or view or meaning before we can experience the impact of the work, but it does go to say that it is implicit in the work and is having its effect upon us in immediate aesthetic terms. Furthermore, in regard to the particular work in question, I do not feel that it is obscure. If anything, the dreamlike effect in many of the stories seems to result from the author's undertaking to squeeze meaning from the item which, in ordinary realistic fiction, would be passed over with a casual glance. Hence the portentousness, the retardation, the otherworldliness. For Miss Welty is like the girl in "A Memory":

> ...from any observation I would conclude that a secret of life had been nearly revealed to me, and from the smallest gesture of

stranger I would wrest what was to me a communication or a pre-
sentiment.

In many cases, as a matter of fact, Miss Welty has heavily edi-
torialized her fiction. She wants us to get that smallest gesture,
to participate in her vision of things as intensely meaningful. And
so there is almost always a gloss to the fable.

One more word: It is quite possible that Miss Welty has pushed
her method to its most extreme limit. It is also possible that the
method, if pursued much farther, would lead to monotony and
self-imitation and merely decorative elaboration. Perhaps we
shall get a fuller drama when her vision is submitted more dar-
ingly to fact, when the definition is plunged into the devouring
river. But meanwhile Miss Welty has given us stories of bril-
liance and intensity; and as for the future, Miss Welty is a writer
of great resourcefulness, sensitivity, and intelligence, and can
probably fend for herself.

Introduction to *Everything That Rises Must Converge*

by Robert Fitzgerald

I

She was a girl who started with a gift for cartooning and satire, and found in herself a far greater gift, unique in her time and place, a marvel. She kept going deeper (this is a phrase she used) until making up stories became, for her, a way of testing and defining and conveying that superior knowledge that must be called religious. It must be called religious but with no false note in our voices, because her writing will make any false note that is applied to it very clear indeed. Bearing hard upon motives and manners, her stories as moralities cut in every direction and sometimes go to the bone of regional and social truth. But we are not likely to state what they show as well as they show it. We can stay on the safe side by affirming, what is true and usefully borne in mind, that making up stories was her craft, her pleasure and her vocation, that her work from first to last is imaginative writing, often comic writing, superbly achieved and always to be enjoyed as that. We had better let our awareness of the knowledge in her stories grow quietly without forcing it, for nothing could be worse than to treat them straight off as problems for exegesis or texts to preach on.

II

The new severely cut slab of marble bearing her name and the dates March 25, 1925—August 3, 1964 lies in the family plot on a bare elevated place in the Milledgeville cemetery, beside another slab of identical shape marking the grave of her father, but his has also a soldier's headstone for Edward F. O'Connor, Jr., Lt. 325th Infantry, 82nd Division, who died February 1st, 1941. I have been out there with her mother to note it all and to say my heart's prayer as I should, though generally I feel as I gather Flannery felt about cemeteries, that they and all they contain are just as well left in God's keeping and that one had better commune with persons, living or dead, than with gravestones and the silent earth. Milledgeville on a mild winter day without leafiness or bloom suggests no less remarkably than in the dogwood season (when I came before) the strict amenity of the older South, or at least this is what I make of there being so many pillared white houses. It was, after all, the capital of Georgia until after the War Between the States.

At the Cline house in town I have been out on the front porch, hatless and coatless in the sun, between the solid handcarved columns, fluted and two stories high, that were hoisted in place when the house was built in 1820 and the slaves, they say, were making by hand the bricks for the house and the openwork walls around the garden. Peter Cline acquired this place in 1886. He was a prominent man, in our American phrase, for many years mayor of the town, and he married successively two sisters, Kate L. and Margaret Ida Treanor. By the former he had seven children and by the latter nine, of whom Regina, Flannery's mother, was the seventh. All of these people were old Georgia Catholics. The first Mass in Milledgeville had been celebrated in the apartment of Hugh Treanor, father of Kate and Ida, in the Newell Hotel in 1847. Mrs. Hugh Treanor gave the plot of ground for the little church that was built in 1874.

From the house in town to the farm called Andalusia is about five miles on the Eatonton-Atlanta highway. A quarter of a mile off the road on rising ground, the white farmhouse looks narrow and steeply roofed with a screen porch across the front of it and a white watertank on very tall stilts behind. The driveway cuts through a red clay bank and curves gently uphill until it swerves around back of the house where there is a roof running out from over the kitchen door to make a broad shelter, and beyond this here are three cedar trees, one with a strong straight bough about eight feet off the grass. The grass is sleeted white by droppings from the peacocks that roost at night on the bough. In the background off to the left is the low darkly weathered clapboard house with a low open porch where the Negroes live and beyond it the barn with farm machinery in the yard. From the carport you see geese going by in single file and there are swans preening in the middle distance; you also see the peacocks proceeding sedate and dainty through the shrubbery to denude it of berries and through the flowerbeds to denude them of buds. There are maybe a dozen or twenty peacocks in sight, fabulous in throat and crest, to say nothing of the billowy tensile train behind. Between the fowls of this farmyard and the writings of Flannery O'Connor, who bought and cared for them and loved to look at them, I do not at all mind drawing a certain parallel, to wit, that if you miss the beauty of plain geese the peacocks will knock your eye out.

I have been in the dining-room looking at old photographs with Regina. There is a big one of Flannery at about two, in profile, sitting crosslegged on a bed and frowning at a large book with an elegantly curled page lit within by reflected light. There is another of her father, a robust amused young man, looking very much the Legion Commander that he was, sitting like the hub of a wheel with his five gay younger brothers beside and behind him. They were a Savannah family, the O'Connors, and Ed, as Flannery always called him, had been in the real estate business there, and Flannery was born and lived her childhood there in a tall narrow brownstone house, going to St. Vincent's parochial school and later to the Sacred Heart. There is a studio photograph of the child at five or six, standing on a bench beside her mother, who is an absolute beauty with a heartshaped face and large grey eyes and dark hair smoothly drawn down from the part. That would be about 1930 or '31 in Savannah. They moved to the Cline house in Milledgeville toward the end of the decade when Mr. O'Connor was ill with a fatal disease called lupus for which no effective treatment was then known. Flannery in her turn would suffer it and die of it or its consequences.

I have also been in the front room on the other side of the house Flannery's bedroom, where she worked. Her aluminum crutches acquired in 1955, are standing against the mantel. The bed is narrow and covered by a plain spread. It has a tall severe wooden headboard. At the foot is one of those moveable tray stands used in hospitals. On the low table to the right of the bed there is a small pile of books covered in black leather, three books in all, on top a Sunday missal, below that a breviary, below that a Holy Bible. To the left of the bed is her work desk, facing away from the front windows, facing the back of a wardrobe that is shoved up against it, no doubt to give her as nearly as possible nothing to look at while she worked. Behind it on a table under the window is a new electric typewriter still unused, still in the corklight plastic box it came in. There are a lot of books in plain bookcases of various sizes around the interior walls. Her painting of a rooster's angry head, on a circular wooden plaque, glares from the top of the tallest bookcase.

In the hall, in the dining-room, and in the comfortable small living-room of the "addition" they built in 1959, the paintings on the walls are all Flannery's, all done during the last thirteen years when she lived, in more or less infirmity, at the farm. They are simple but beautiful paintings of flowers in bowls, of cows under trees, of the Negro house under the bare trees of winter. I use this word "beautiful" with all possible premeditation. Once when I was working at a university I was asked with a couple of my friends who taught there to take part in a symposium on Flannery's work, a symposium which I expected would be favorable if critical, but it turned out that one of my friends didn't like her work at all because he thought it lacked a sense of natural beauty and human beauty. Troubled by this, I looked in the stories again and took a sentence from "The Artificial Nigger" to say what I felt she perceived not only in natural things but in her characters: "The trees were full of silver-white sunlight, and even the meanest of them sparkled." Surely even the meanest of them do. I observed that in the violent tale called "A Good Man is Hard to Find" the least heroic of the characters was able, on his way to be shot, to shout a reassurance to his mother (though supporting himself against a tree) and that his wife, asked if she would like to follow him, murmured "Yes, thank you," as she got up with her baby and her broken shoulder. These were beautiful actions, I argued, though as brief as beautiful actions usually are.

To come back to the paintings, they are not only skilled in the application of paint but soundly composed and bold and sensitive in color and revelatory of their subjects, casual as the whole business was for her. She went deeper in this art as well. I know because I have looked through a sheaf of drawings she made before she was twenty when she was going to the Georgia Woman's College in Milledgeville and doing linoleum cut cartoons for the college paper, *Colonnade.* In one of the sketches one fish is saying to another, "You can go jump out of the lake," an idea in which I can hear, already, the authentic O'Connor humor. In the linoleum cuts the line was always strong and decisive with an energy and angularity that recall the pen drawings of George Price, drawings that in fact she admired. For the yearbook, *Spectrum,* for 1945, when she graduated, she tried a rounder kind of comic drawing, not so good. She was editor of the literary magazine, *The Corinthian,* that year and so clearly on her way to being a writer that one of her teachers took the initiative in getting her a fellowship to the Writers' Workshop at the University of Iowa. She began to publish before she got her M.A. there in 1947. After one more year at Iowa, she worked on her writing at Yaddo and in New York. ...

V

The black sky was underpinned with long silver streaks that looked like scaffolding and depth on depth behind it were thousands of stars that all seemed to be moving very slowly as if they were about some vast construction work that involved the whole order of the universe and would take all time to complete. No one was paying any attention to the sky. The stores in Taulkinham stayed open on Thursday nights so that people could have an extra opportunity to see what was for sale.

(Wise Blood)

A catchword when Flannery O'Connor began to write was the German *angst,* and it seemed that Auden had hit it off in one of his titles as the "Age of Anxiety." The last word in attitudes was the Existentialist one, resting on the perception that beyond any immediate situation there is possibly nothing—nothing beyond, nothing behind, nada. Now, our country family in 1949 and 1950 believed on excellent grounds that beyond the immediate there was practically everything, like the stars over Taulkinham—the past, the future, and the Creater thereof. But the horror of recent human predicaments had not been lost on us. Flannery felt that an artist who was a Catholic should face all the truth down to the worst of it. If she worried about the side effects of the ungenteel imagination, she took heart that year from Mauriac's dictum about "purifying the source"—the creative spirit—rather than damming or diverting the stream.

In *Wise Blood* she did parody the Existentialist point of view, as Brainard Cheney has said (in the *Sewanee Review* for Autumn, 1964), but the parody was very serious. In this and in most of her later writing she gave to the godless a force proportionate to the force it actually has: in episode after episode, as in the world, as in ourselves, it wins. We can all hear our disbelief, picked out of the air we breathe, when Hazel Motes says, "I'm going to preach there was no Fall because there was nothing to fall from and no Redemption because there was no Fall and no Judgment because there wasn't the first two. Nothing matters but that Jesus was a liar." And in whom is *angst* so dead that he never feels, as Haze puts it: "Where you came from is gone, where you thought you were going to never was there, and where you are is no good unless you can get away from it."

Note the velocity and rightness of these sentences. Many pages and a number of stories by this writer have the same perfection, and the novels have it in sections though they narrowly miss it as wholes. I am speaking now of merits achieved in the reader's interest: no unliving words, the realization of character by exquisitely chosen speech and interior speech and behavior, the action moving at the right speed so that no part of the situation is left out or blurred and the violent thing, though surprising, happens after due preparation, because it has to. Along with her gifts, patient toil and discipline brought about these merits, and a further question can be asked about that: Why? What was the standard to which the writer felt herself answerable? Well, in 1957 she said:

"The serious fiction writer will think that any story that can be entirely explained by the adequate motivation of the characters or by a believable imitation of a way of life or by a proper theology, will not be a large enough story for him to occupy himself with. This is not to say that he doesn't have to be concerned with adequate motivation or accurate reference or a right theology; he does; but he has to be concerned with them only because the meaning of his story does not begin except at a depth where these things have been exhausted. The fiction writer presents mystery through manners, grace through nature, but when he finishes, there always has to be left over that sense of Mystery which cannot be accounted for by any human formula."

This is an open and moving statement of a certain end for literary art. The end, and some of the terms used here, seem to me similar to those of another Christian writer who died recently, T.S. Eliot. I do not propose any confusion between a London man of letters who wrote verse and criticism and a Southern woman who wrote fiction, for indeed they lived a world apart. Only at the horizon, one might say, do the lines each pursued come together; but the horizon is an important level. It is also important that they were similarly moved toward serious art, being early and much possessed by death as a reality, a strong spiritual sensation, giving odd clarity to the appearances they saw through or saw beyond. In her case as in his, if anyone at first found the writing startling he could pertinently remind himself how startling it was going to be to lose his own body, that Ancient Classic. Sensibility in both produced a wariness of beautiful letters and, in the writing, a concision of effect.

When it comes to seeing the skull beneath the skin, we may remark that the heroes of both O'Connor novels are so perceived within the first few pages, and her published work begins and ends with coffin dreams. Her *memento mori* is no less authentic for being often hilarious, devastating to a secular world and all it cherishes. The O'Connor equivalent for Eliot's drowned Phoenician sailor ("Consider Phlebas, who was once handsome and tall as you") is a museum piece, the shrunken corpse that the idiot Enoch Emery in *Wise Blood* proposes as the new humanist jesus.

> "See theter notice," Enoch said in a church whisper, pointing to a typewritten card at the man's foot, "it says he was once as tall as you or me. Some A-rabs did it to him in six months..."

And there is a classic exchange in "The Life You Save May Be Your Own":

> "Why listen, lady," said Mr. Shiftlet with a grin of delight, "the monks of old slept in their coffins."
> "They wasn't as advanced as we are," the old woman said.

The state of being as advanced as we are had been, of course, blasted to glory in *The Waste Land* before Flannery made her version, a translation, as it were, into American ("The Vacant Lot"). To take what used to be called low life and picture it as farcically empty, raging with energy, and at the same time, *sub specie aeternitatis,* full of meaning: this was the point of *Sweeney Agonistes* and the point of many pages of O'Connor. As for our monuments, those of a decent godless people, surely the asphalt road and the thousand lost golf balls are not a patch on images like that of the hillside covered with used car bodies, in *The Violent Bear It Away:*

> In the indistinct darkness, they seemed to be drowning into the ground, to be about half-submerged already. The city hung in front of them on the side of the mountain as if it were a larger part of the same pile, not yet buried so deep. The fire had gone out of it and it appeared settled into its unbreakable parts.

Death is not the only one of the Last Things present in the O'Connor stories; Judgment is there, too. On the pride of contemporary man, in particular on flying as his greatest achievement, Tarwater in *The Violent* has a prophet's opinion:

> "I wouldn't give you nothing for no airplane. A buzzard can fly."

Christ the tiger, a phrase in Eliot, is a force felt in O'Connor. So is the impulse to renounce the blessèd face, and to renounce the voice. In her work we are shown that vices are fathered by our heroism, virtues forced upon us by our impudent crimes, and that neither fear nor courage saves us (we are saved by grace, if at all, though courage may dispose us toward grace). Her best stories do the work that Eliot wished his plays to do, raising anagogical meaning over literal action. He may have felt this himself, for though he rarely read fiction I am told that a few years before he died he read her stories and exclaimed in admiration at them.

VI

The title of the present book comes from Teilhard de Chardin, whose works Flannery O'Connor had been reading at least since early 1961 when she recommended them to me. It is a title taken in full respect and with profound and necessary irony. For Teilhard's vision of the "omega point" virtually at the end of time, or at any rate of a time-span rightly conceivable by paleontologist or geologist alone, has appealed to people to whom it may seem to offer one more path past the Crucifixion. That could be corrected by no sense of life better than by O'Connor's. Quite as austere in its way as his, her vision will hold us down to earth where the clashes of blind wills and the low dodges of the heart permit any rising or convergence only at the cost of agony. At that cost, yes, a little.

The better a poem or piece of fiction, the more corrective or indeed destructive it is likely to be of any fatuous happiness in abstractions. "Rising" and "convergence" in these stories, as the title story at once makes clear, are shown in classes, generations, and colors. What each story has to say is what it shows. If we are aware that the meaning of the stories is to be sought in the stories and well apprehended in the stories alone, we may try a few rough and cautious statements about them. Thus the title story shows, amid much else in a particular action of particular persons, young and old and black and white to be practically sealed off against one another, struggling but hardly upward or together in a welter of petty feelings and cross purposes, resolved only slightly even by the tragic blow. "Slightly," however, may mean a great deal in the economy of this writer. The story is one of those, like "The Artificial Nigger" in her first collection and "Revelation" in this, in which the low-keyed and calibrated style is allowed a moment of elevation.

What is wrong in this story we feel to be diffused throughout the persons and in the predicament itself, but in at least two of the stories, and those among the latest and most elaborate, the malign is more concentrated in one personage. I do not mean *il maligno*, as the Italians call the devil. There are few better representations of the devil in fiction that Tarwater's friend, as overheard and finally embodied in *The Violent;* but in these two stories, "The Comforts of Home" and "The Lame Shall Enter First," the personage in question is not quite that. He need not be, since the souls to be attacked are comparatively feeble. Brainless and brainy depravity are enough, respectively, to bring down in ruin an irritable academic and a self-regarding do-gooder. The latter story is clearly a second effort with the three figures of the novel, Tarwater, Rayber and Bishop, who are here reworked, more neatly in some respects, as Johnson, Shepard and Norton.

Other similarities link various stories to one another and to earlier stories. There is a family resemblance between Julian in the title story, Wesley in "Greenleaf," Ashbury in "The Enduring Chill" and Thomas in "The Comforts of Home." The Wellesley girl in "Revelation" is related to all these and to the girl in "Good Country People." In the various mothers of the stories there are facets of Mrs. McIntyre in "The Displaced Person." Parker in "Parker's Back" has some of the traits of a latter-day Hazel Motes. The critic will note these recurrent types and situations. He will note too that the setting remains the same, Southern and rural as he will say, and that large classes of contemporary experience, as of industry and war and office work and foreign travel, are barely touched if touched at all. But in saying how the stories are limited and how they are not, the sensitive critic will have a care. For one thing, it is evident that the writer deliberately and indeed indifferently, almost defiantly, restricted her horizontal range; a pasture scene and a fortress wall of pine woods reappear like a signature in story after story. The same is true of her social range and range of idiom. But these restrictions, like the very humility of her style, are all deceptive. The true range of the stories is vertical and Dantesque in what is taken in, in scale of implication. As to the style, there is also more to say.

She would be sardonic over the word *ascesis,* but it seems to me a good one for the peculiar discipline of the O'Connor style. How much has been refrained from, and how much else has been cut out and thrown away, in order that the bald narrative sentences should present just what they present and in just this order! What counts is the passion by which the stories were formed, the depth, as Virginia Woolf said of Milton, at which the options were taken. Beyond incidental phrasing and images, beauty lies in the strong invention and execution of the things, as in objects expertly forged or cast or stamped, with edges, not waxen and worn or softly moulded.

If we look for pleasure of a secondary kind such as we take in the shadings and suffusions of Henry James, I suggest that this is given in these stories by the comedy. There is quite a gamut of it, running from something very like cartooning to an irony dry and refined, especially in the treatment of the most serious matters. John Crowe Ransom was the first reader known to me to realize and say that Flannery O'Connor was one of our few tragic writers, a fact that we will not miss now in reading "The Displaced Person" in the first volume or "The Comforts of Home" in this. But it is far from the whole story. On the tragic scene, each time, the presence of her humor is like the presence of grace. Has not tragicomedy at least since Dante been the most Christian of *genres?*

I do not want to claim too much for these stories, or to imply that every story comes off equally well. That would be unfaithful to her own conscience and sense of fact. Let the good critic rejoice in the field for discrimination these stories offer him. Before I turn them over to him and to the reader, I should like to offer a reflection or two on the late masterpiece called "Revelation." One of its excellences is to present through a chance collection in a doctor's waiting room a picture of a whole "section" —realized, that is, in the human beings who compose it, each marvelously and irreducibly what he or she is. For one example of the rendering, which is faultless, consider this:

> A grotesque revolving shadow passed across the curtain behind her and was thrown palely on the opposite wall. Then a bicycle clattered down against the outside of the building. The door opened and a colored boy glided in with a tray from the drug store. It had two large red and white paper cups on it with tops on them. He was a tall, very black boy in discolored white pants and a green nylon shirt. He was chewing gum slowly, as if to music. He set the tray down in the office opening next to the fern and stuck his head through to look for the secretary. She was not in there. He rested his arm on the ledge and waited, his narrow bottom stuck out, swaying slowly to the left and right. He raised a hand over his head and scratched the base of his skull.

Not only do we see this boy for the rest of our lives; for an instant we hear him think. But the greater excellence of the story is to bring about a rising and a convergence, a movement of spirit in Ruby Turpin that is her rising to a terrible occasion, and a convergence between her and the violent agent of this change.

The terms of the struggle are intensely local, as they will be in all such struggles, but we need not be too shy about seeing through them to the meaning that lies beyond at the usual mys-

terious depth. How else but at a mysterious depth can we understand a pretty notion like the Soul of the South? What the struggle
requires of Mrs. Turpin is courage and humility, that is clear
enough. Perhaps as a reward for these, her eyes are opened. And
the ascent that she sees at the end, in an astonishment like the
astonishment of the new dead, takes place against that field of
stars that moved beyond Taulkinham in *Wise Blood* and that
hold for a small boy, in another of these stories, the lost presence
of his mother.

Flannery O'Connor, a Realist of Distances

by Sister M. Bernetta Quinn, O.S.F.
College of Saint Teresa

Brainard Cheney, in a *Sewanee Review* tribute, has called Flannery O'Connor the most significant fiction writer in our time despite the slender volume she left to American letters.[1] Miss O'Connor's stock, like that of John Fitzgerald Kennedy, has tremendously increased in value since her death. Her importance in contemporary criticism can be ascribed to her prophetic vision as expressed in highly individualized invention. She herself saw vividly the relationship between prophecy and fiction. Once she told a college audience: "The prophet is a realist of distances, and it is this kind of realism which goes into great novels. It is a realism which does not hesitate to distort appearances in order to show a hidden truth."[2]

Although *prophet* comes from the Greek *prophetes,* "to speak before," prophets are first of all forthtellers, not foretellers. They understand the present, enunciating their inspired insights before the ordinary man sees more than the surface level. They are men who deliver divine messages or interpret the divine will.[3] Miss O'Connor identifies with her special talent two very closely re-

Extracted from "Flannery O'Connor, a Realist of Distances" by Sister M. Bernetta Quinn, O.S.F. Reprinted by permission of the publisher from *The Added Dimension:* The Art and Mind of Flannery O'Connor, edited by Melvin Friedman and Lewis A. Lawson (2nd edition) (New York: Fordham University Press, 1977). Copyright © 1977 by Fordham University Press, pp. 157-167.

[1]"Flannery O'Connor's Campaign for Her Country," *Sewanee Review,* LXXII (Autumn, 1964), 555.
[2]"The Role of the Catholic Novelist," *Greyfriar* [Siena Studies in Literature], VII (1964), 9.
[3]*Funk and Wagnall's Standard College Dictionary* (New York: Funk and Wagnall, 1963), p. 1080.

lated words: *vision* and *revelation*. *Vision,* from the past participle *videre,* refers to a mental representation of external objects as in a religious revelation or dream. Such might be any transfiguration of the material world as found in Miss O'Connor's work. *Revelation,* a key term in her fiction, is the title of a short story published the spring before she died.[4] Considered as an *unveiling (re-*back, *velum-*veil), it means to make visible, to show. To return to *prophet,* a synonym is *seer,* linking all four words.

One article on Flannery O'Connor makes the above identification explicit in its title, "Prophet in the Wilderness."[5] Silenced by death in August, 1964, the voice crying in the wilderness is at last getting its hearing. The Archbishop of Atlanta, the Most Reverend Paul Hallinan, in giving her funeral sermon, expressed the idea that to the artist as well as to the mother, nurse, social worker, and other equally obvious examples belongs the reward promised in St. Matthew, XXV: "Whatever you did for the least of these you did for Me." Miss O'Connor was fully aware of the God-given nature of her mission. As she tole one journalist: "There is the prophetic sense of 'seeing through' reality and there is also the prophetic function of recalling people to known but ignored truths."[6]

Flannery O'Connor's faith enlarged her universe, gave it an added dimension, enabled her through Scripture study to penetrate reality. It is best to state this truth in her own words: "In the novelist's case, it is a matter of seeing near things with their extensions of meaning and thus of seeing far things close up."[7] What this meant, practically, for her craft, was that she, herself a prophet, had to create prophets. These characters are to do for reality what the Biblical prophets did: impart a fuller significance to what everyone experiences. They are not among those whom Eliot mentions in the *Four Quartets:* "We had the experience but missed the meaning."

To recall people to ignored truths, Miss O'Connor, writing in a materialistic age, sometimes had to shout, that is, to exaggerate. Perhaps this is why certain readers tend to think of her fiction as

[4]*Sewanee Review,* LXXII (Spring, 1964), 178-202.
[5]Sister Bede Sullivan, *Today,* XV (March, 1960), 36.
[6]Joel Wells, "Off the Cuff," *Critic,* XXI (August-September, 1962), 72.
[7]"The Role of the Catholic Novelist," p. 9.

gloomy and morbid, whereas actually her optimism decidedly outweighs her pessimism: more often than not, her distorted figures respond to prophecy and amend their lives. The same fruitful outcome of the prophet's warning in the Old Testament times is stressed by Father Carroll Stuhlmueller in *The Prophets and the Word of God:* "God's word, heard through the voice of the prophets, not only shattered rocks of stubbornness and prejudice, but it also pulled down mountains of pride and turned the rugged terrain of persecution into the broad valley of peace."[8] This quotation is a perfect summary of the effect in Flannery O'Connor's own favorite among her short stories, "The Artificial Nigger."

En route to show his grandson Nelson the city, Mr. Head reveals himself as smugly proud. Although he himself does not realize this pride, the prophetic author does as she constructs her symbolic parable. Once in the city, he puts a penny in a public weight machine and believes the description on the card to be quite accurate ("You are upright and brave and all your friends admire you"), while disregarding the fact that the weight figure, 120 pounds, is entirely wrong. After he denies knowing his grandson when the latter gets into an embarrassing scrape, he feels all the pangs of Judas until he obtains the boy's forgiveness when they encounter an object both are ignorant of: an artificial nigger decorating someone's yard.

That night, when the train slows down to let them off at their home town, Mr. Head undergoes an epiphany which links him to what Albert Schweitzer has called "the brotherhood of pain":

> Mr. Head stood very still and felt the action of mercy touch him again but this time he knew that there were no words in the world that could name it. He understood that it grew out of agony, which is not denied to any man and which is given in strange ways to children. He understood it was all a man could carry into death to give his Maker and he suddenly burned with shame that he had so little of it to take with him (213).

Mr. Head, a surname reminiscent of Hawthorne's dichotomy, has discovered what it means to be human.

The grandson also has seen deeply into reality: in this symbolic story Miss O'Connor does for Nelson what Sherwood Ander-

son does for his sixteen-year-old hero in "I Want to Know Why."
Both boys are initiated into evil. During his day in the city Nelson
has looked into a sewer hole "and understood for the first time
how the world was put together in its lower parts" (204). But the
experience climaxing in the "vision" of the artificial nigger has
left both him and his betrayer (perhaps more fittingly compared
to Peter as Head of the Church than to Judas) advanced in wisdom
and rooted in charity. . . .

Typical of the greater sympathy for human frailty evident in
her later stories (each characterized more by "a Damascus Road
experience, perhaps, rather than a consuming vision of judgment")[9] are "The Comforts of Home" and "The Partridge Festi-
val." Thomas, nicknamed Tomsee, in the first and Calhoun in
the second are instances of persons who through grace, especially
when this takes a violent form, see the consequences of their actions and undergo conversion, or *metanoia*. The vision in both
cases results in light, not darkness.

In "The Comforts of Home" Thomas, an apostle of mediocrity,
does not believe in the devil. If he has any religion, his credo
centers around his personal *status quo*. From a cruel, corrupt
father, Thomas has inherited a dearth of compassion. When his
mother rescues from prison and brings home a nymphomaniac,
Thomas keeps insulting the girl, among other ways by calling her
Sarah rather than Star, as she has renamed herself from a motive
just the reverse of Joy Hopewell's in calling herself Hulga ("Good
Country People"). His rejection of the Biblical practice of name-
changing is indicative of his secularism. Irony glitters in the fact
that *Star* recalls the Epiphany, with its radiance drawing others
to Christ, whereas Star herself (to Thomas, at least) had the appearance of the blind who don't know they are blind. Her pet
name for him, Tomsee, is also ironic, when there is so much that
he definitely does not see. In the story he is compared to non-
human creatures: a bull, a turtle. His lack of faith, except in the
"virtue" of moderation, contrasts with Star's belief in God, the
devil, and hell, even though she despairs of salvation.

As is frequent in Miss O'Connor's fiction, when the characters
are forced to realize through an epiphany the vile results of their
actions, they undergo a reformation. In "The Comforts of Home"

[9]Robert Drake, "The Harrowing Evangel of Flannery O'Connor," *Christian
Century*, LXXXI (September 30, 1964), 1200.

(as wonderfully satiric a title as most in the two collections), this change as it is occurring is seen through the eyes of the sheriff, comically named Farebrother though he is anything but fair or brotherly:

> As he scrutinized the scene, further insights were flashed to him. Over her body, the killer and the slut were about to collapse into each other's arms. The sheriff knew a nasty bit when he saw it. He was accustomed to enter upon scenes that were not as bad as he had hoped to find them, but this one met his expectations (*Everything*, 141-42).

Whatever the sheriff or others may think, Thomas's mother has not died in vain. Thomas has put his hand into the Lord's wounded side....

Probably the best example of grace in action, of prophecy falling like good seed on good ground, is "A Temple of the Holy Ghost." It comes to us as a series of happenings perceived by a very human little girl. Her mind wanders, as ours all do, and she combines fervor with indifference: mischievous, yet at the same time devout. What Hemingway effects so well in *The Sun Also Rises* is also present here: Nature with its "gathering greenness," "dark woods," and the red ball of the sun is contrasted with the triviality and even the evil of humanity (the girl's silly cousins). Since the whole pattern of images, taken out of the thought-processes of the child, is Catholic, the sun as Host does not strike one as so out of place as it does in the famous passage from Crane's *The Red Badge of Courage*. When asked by student reviewers during her 1960 stay in Winona, Minnesota, why the sun is a common image in her stories, Miss O'Connor answered: "It's there. It's so obvious. And from time immemorial it's been a god."[10]

One gets the impression that "A Temple of the Holy Ghost" is another initiation story, such as "I Want to Know Why." The child knows that she is in the presence of evil but cannot understand it. However, her experience, unlike the incidents in the Sherwood Anderson story, is related to an eternal dimension. With genuine humility the child recognizes her faults, to her as

[10]Katherine Fugin, Faye Rivard, and Margaret Sieh, "An Interview with Flannery O'Connor," *Censer* (Fall, 1960), 30.

serious as the sins of her elders, but makes reparation for them by a vehement rejection of the sordid in life and by regret for her impatient, uncharitable behavior. In the end, not only the girl but the world itself becomes the temple of the Holy Ghost.

Miss O'Connor, however, can and repeatedly does highlight the negative, despite these examples of a positive response to the divine invitation. She looks at her world with wide-open eyes and speaks about both the crude and the ugly, as did Christ in His parables, and she avoids any sentimental, *deus ex machina* endings. Her most celebrated story, "A Good Man Is Hard to Find," illustrates these traits. Her distortions are intended to "break through" to those who see the grotesque as normal (e.g., exponents of racism in twentieth-century America or the adulation of entertainment stars). Unlike Anderson's use of the grotesque, whereby one truth is stressed at the expense of Truth itself, Flannery O'Connor's grotesques correspond to dictionary meanings of the word: *distorted* (and we think of the one-legged atheist Hulga); *incongruous* (Hazel Motes with his queer hat in *Wise Blood*); *ugly in appearance* (Sabbath Lily in the same novel). A secondary meaning of *grotesque* refers to fantastic combinations of human and animal figures. One regular feature of Miss O'Connor's style is picturing human beings in terms of animal imagery: *large bug, wheezing horse, hyena, sheep, crab, goat, dog, buzzard, monkey.* Sometimes she goes almost as far as Steinbeck in this technique, although no concept of the nature of man could be more different than his from hers. Whereas he builds his fiction on a deterministic basis, she underscores above all the freedom of the will. It is the latter which makes her stories so very exciting for those who see: the high stakes elevate the trivial to cosmic proportions.

The reason she often chooses grotesques is that these are the characters she can make live. She believes in the parable of the talents as related by Christ. Writing in *The Living Novel,* she asserts that all initial gifts are from God, and not even the least must be destroyed by using it outside its proper sphere.[11] Almost all her characters are either evangelical Protestants or men without faith; living in Milledgeville, Georgia, located in the Bible Belt, Flannery O'Connor knew best these people and their

[11]"The Fiction Writer and His Country," in *The Living Novel, a Symposium,* edited by Granville Hicks (New York: Macmillan, 1957), pp. 158-59.

conscious or unconscious distortions of the face of Christ. Catholicism is a minority report in her environment. "The Enduring Chill," a *Harper's Bazaar* story (1958),[12] was the first specifically Catholic fiction she ever published. In *The Living Novel*, Miss O'Connor makes the statement: "My own feeling is that writers who see by the light of their Christian faith will have, in these times, the sharpest eyes for the grotesque, for the perverse, and for the unacceptable."[13]

The prophecies Catholics are most familiar with are the ones prefiguring Christ: the Books of Isaiah and Daniel. Miss O'Connor concentrates on the less-publicized prophets (Amos, Osee, Jonah, Obadiah) who endeavored to make their contemporaries see how far they were departing from what God wanted. Each had his own individuality, and yet they tend in our imaginations to join their voices under the typical term *prophet*. Men like Jeremiah were flesh and blood, real people, not just names on a scroll or printed page. Flannery O'Connor's characters also have this two-fold identity, the individual and the type. James G. Murray, writing for *The Critic*, says: "They have the look of people who walk on earth, and yet their voice is one of prophecy—the kind of prophecy which derives from a penetrating absorption in, not a divorcement or alienation from, this world."[14]

"Parker's Back," the last story by Miss O'Connor to appear in magazine form,[15] may prove in time her very greatest. O.E. Parker, upon fiery cross-examination by the woman he is courting, turns out to be Obadiah Elihue: Obadiah, after the sixth-century B.C. minor prophet, and Elihue after Elihu, a visitor to Job in the thirty-second chapter of that account. As is not unusual in this writer, O.E. fails to convert the heathen but himself undergoes an everlasting metamorphosis. His wife (they eventually do marry, though he cannot see how he ever came to find himself bound to so repulsive a person as Sarah Ruth Cates) forever flings the judgment of God in his face and scorns the one

[12]*Harper's Bazaar*, XCI (July, 1958), 44-45, 94, 96, 100-02, 108.

[13]"The Fiction Writer and His Country," p. 162. Miss O'Connor connects this insight with prophecy by stating on the next page: "Those who believe that art proceeds from a healthy, and not from a diseased, faculty of the mind will take what he [the artist] shows them as a revelation...under given circumstances; that is, as a limited revelation but a revelation nevertheless."

[14]"Southland *à la Russe*," *Critic*, XXI (June-July, 1963), 27.

[15]*Esquire*, LXIII (April, 1965), 76-78, 151-55.

thing which nourishes his ego: his collection of tattoos covering his whole body except for his back, where, since he could not see them, [they] would give him no pleasure. He decides to add a religious tattoo in this undecorated area, to interest his highly moral wife. Before selecting the design, O.E. is given his apocalyptic vision, one which comes upon him as he is baling hay on the farm where he does day-labor for an elderly woman:

> As he circled the field his mind was on a suitable design for his back. The sun, the size of a golf ball, began to switch regularly from in front to behind him, but he appeared to see it both places as if he had eyes in the back of his head. All at once he saw the tree reaching out to grasp him. A ferocious thud propelled him into the air, and he heard himself yelling in an unbelievably loud voice, "GOD ABOVE!" (*Everything*, 232).

The tractor, his shoes, and the tree burst into flame. "Parker did not allow himself to think on the way to the city. He only knew that there had been a great change in his life, a leap forward into a worse unknown, and that there was nothing the could do about it" (*Everything*, 233).

No drawing in the artist's collection suits him except the face of a Byzantine Christ, which pulls him toward its magnetic, "all-demanding eyes," insistent that it be chosen. Even after the vision described above, O.E. fails to acknowledge any need for Redemption. To the artist's query as to whether he has "got religion," he says bitterly: "A man can't save his self from whatever it is he don't deserve none of my sympathy" (*Everything*, 238). The men in the pool hall to which he goes are eager to see O.E.'s new decoration and yank off his shirt; in the fight that follows a weird silence, during which they gaze incredulously at the face of Christ, Obadiah Elihue lashes out at the scoffers as fearlessly as might the sternest of Old Testament prophets. "Then a calm descended on the pool hall as nerve-shattering as if the long barn-like room were the ship from which Jonah had been cast into the sea" (*Everything*, 241).

Perhaps it is this episode of violence that turns the main character toward a perception of the truth. As he sits on the ground in the alley behind the pool hall, he examines the "spider web of facts and lies" that is his soul. He discovers that he belongs to Christ: "The eyes that were now forever on his back were eyes to be obeyed. He was as certain of it as he had ever been of anything"

(*Everything*, 241). Love plays no part in this certainty. Driving home, he finds the familiar countryside entirely strange and himself alien to it. Until he whispers through the keyhole his prophet's name, his shrew of a wife will not open the locked door. When she does, instead of recognizing the fresh tattoo as a picture of God, she begins to beat him over the shoulders with a broom, screaming at him that she will have no idolator in her house. The closing sentence suggests a crucifixion scene: "There he was— who called himself Obadiah Elihue—leaning against the tree, crying like a baby" (*Everything*, 244).

In "Parker's Back," as in other stories, prophecy is equated with fire. Writing to the author about this identification in January, 1960, Miss O'Connor said:

> I have been reading what St. Thomas has to say in the *De Veritate* on prophecy. He says prophecy depends on the imaginative and not the moral faculty. It's a matter of seeing. Those who, like Tarwater, see, will see what they have no desire to see and the vision will be the purifying fire. I think I am not done with prophets.[16]

Prophecy like poetry is often symbolic to a marked degree; there was very little imagination in Sarah Ruth Parker, and there is very little in many another character created by Miss O'Connor to contrast with her prophets and those imaginative enough to enter with good will into the purifying fire, a fire corresponding to Eliot's in *Little Gidding* but even more like that of Dante's great vision in the effect which his purgatorial revelations had on the pilgrim through eternal distances, the distances Miss O'Connor portrays under the guise of temporal realities.

[16]In the same letter Miss O'Connor says: "Baptism is just another idiocy to the general intelligent reader and the idea of anyone's having a vocation to be a prophet doesn't commend itself to his sense of the fitness of things in the 20th century."

The Other Side of Despair

by Thomas Merton

The existentialism which is most active and of most vital interest to the Church today is neither as well publicized nor as thoroughly discussed as the literature of those earlier days [i.e., Camus and the early Sartre—Ed.] : it is the existentialist theology, both Protestant and Catholic, which owes so much to Heidegger.

...Existentialism is an experience and an attitude, rather than a system of thought. As soon as it begins to present itself as a system, it denies and destroys itself. Non-objective, elusive, concrete, dynamic, always in movement and always seeking to renew itself in the newness of the present situation, genuine existentialism is, like Zen Buddhism and like apophatic Christian mysticism, hidden in life itself. It cannot be distilled out in verbal formulas. Above all, the journalistic clichés about existentialist nihilism, pessimism, anarchism, and so on, are totally irrelevant, even though they may have some foundation in certain existentialist writings. It is my contention that these writings cannot fairly be taken as representative of genuine existentialism.

Rather than attempt still another abstract and technical definition of something which, in itself, is neither abstract nor technical, let us begin with a concrete example. Existentialism has expressed itself most unambiguously in literature, where it is free from technicalities and quasi-official formulas. Literature offers us an example quite close to home, in the novels and short stories of Flannery O'Connor. I can think of no American writer who has made a more devastating use of existential intuition. She does so, of course, without declamation, without program, without distributing manifestoes, and without leading a parade. Current existentialism is, in fact, neither partisan nor programmatic. It is content with the austere task of minding its own literary, philosophical, or theological business.

A casual consideration of the "good" and the "bad" people in Flannery O'Connor will help us to appreciate the existentialist point of view—that point of view which is so easily obscured when it presents itself in terms of a program. For example, in her story, "A Good Man Is Hard to Find," evil is not so much in the gangsters, so fatally and so easily "found," as in the garrulous, empty-headed, folksy, sentimental old fool of a grandmother. Not that she is deliberately wicked, but the fact is, she does get everybody killed. It is her absurd and arbitrary fantasy that leads them directly to the "good man" and five deaths. She is a kind of blank, a void through which there speaks and acts the peculiar nemesis that inhabits (or haunts) the world of Flannery O'Connor—and doubtless ours too, if we could but see it as she did. This frightening action of Sophoclean nemesis in and through the right-thinking man who is null and void is spelled out in its full and public identity in types like Rayber, the positivist schoolteacher in *The Violent Bear It Away.*

The first thing that anyone notices in reading Flannery O'Connor is that her moral evaluations seem to be strangely scrambled. The good people are bad and the bad people tend to be less bad than they seem. This is not in itself unusual. But her crazy people, while remaining as crazy as they can possibly be, turn out to be governed by a strange kind of sanity. In the end, it is the sane ones who are incurable lunatics. The "good," the "right," the "kind" do all the harm. "Love" is a force for destruction, and "truth" is the best way to tell a lie.

Rayber is, by all standards, the kind of person our society accepts as normal, not only a sane man but a kind one. A teacher, a man with forward-looking and optimistic perspectives, illuminated and blessed with a scientific world view, he is acquainted with all the best methods for helping people to become happy and well adjusted in the best of all possible societies.

It is he who sees through nonsense, prejudice, and myth. It is he who gets the Bible student to sleep with the frustrated girl from the woods, to relieve her tensions and open her up to a more joyous and fulfilled mode of life. It is he who, when their child is born, wants to protect him against the fanatic uncle, the prophet and believer. It is he who suffers permanent damage (deafness) trying to liberate the boy from the awful trammels of obscurantism and superstition. Rayber is our kind of man, is he not? A sound and practical positivist, well adjusted in a scientific age. True, he is not a Catholic, but we have plenty of Catholics who think more or less as he does, and he could perhaps be persuaded that we too are reasonable.

Yet as we read Flannery O'Connor we find an uncomfortable feeling creeping over us: we are on the side of the fanatic and the mad boy, and we are against this reasonable zombie. We are against everything he stands for. We find ourselves nauseated by the reasonable, objective, "scientific" answers he has for everything. In him, science is so right that it is a disaster.

Such is the dire effect of reading an existentialist.

Rayber wants to help the wild boy to find himself, to forget the madness he learned from the prophet, to become a docile and useful citizen in a world of opportunity where he can at last have everything. Rayber will not count the cost in sacrifice that must be paid. "Now I can make up for all the time we've lost. I can help correct what he's done to you, help you to correct it yourself... This is our problem together."

It was perhaps not kind of the boy, Tarwater, to be so suspicious of the world of reason, psychiatry, and togetherness, or to look with such an ugly glint upon the teacher's hearing aid. ("What you wired for?" he drawled. "Does your head light up?")

Alas, we share his cruel satisfaction. We have come to agree that the positivist Mephistopheles from Teachers College is a pure void, a mouthpiece for demons.

> "I forget what color eyes he's got," the old man would say, irked. "What difference does the color make when I know the look? I know what's behind it."
> "What's behind it?"
> "Nothing. He's full of nothing."
> "He knows a heap," the boy said. "I don't reckon it's anything he don't know."
> "He don't know it's anything he can't know," the old man said. "That's his trouble. He thinks if it's something he can't know then

somebody smarter than him can tell him about it and he can know it just the same. And if you were to go there, the first thing he would do would be to test your head and tell you what you were thinking and how come you were thinking it and what you ought to be thinking instead. And before long you wouldn't belong to yourself no more, you would belong to him."

This, in brief, is the existentialist case against the scientism and sociologism of positivist society. It is a brief for the person and for personal, spiritual liberty against determinism and curtailment.

The old man was doing Rayber no injustice. This is precisely what his *hubris* consists in: the conviction that the infinite rightness and leveling power of "scientific method" has given him a mandate to transform other people into his own image: which is the image of nothing. And though he is "nothing," yet others, he knows it well, must do things his way since he has science on his side.

If, for Flannery O'Connor, the mild, agnostic, and objective teacher is not so much evil as pure void, and if this is what it means to be a villain—this will to reduce everyone else by an infallible process to the same void as oneself—we begin to understand existentialism in its passionate resistance against the positivist outlook. We also begin to see why, after all, existentialism is no immediate danger in a society almost entirely inclined to the consolations of sociometric methods.

Existentialism offers neither attractions nor peril to people who are perfectly convinced that they are headed in the right direction, that they possess the means to attain a reasonably perfect happiness, that they have a divine mandate to remove anyone who seems inclined to interfere with this aim. Existentialism calls into question the validity, indeed the very possibility, of such an aim. But, for positivism, its rightness is never in question. Nor, indeed, is its nature. The positivist does not even need to be quite sure where he is going. The direction must be the right one, since it is determined by his processes and by his scientific method. For him, the only question that really matters is *how* to keep on moving faster and faster in the same direction. Philosophy reduces itself to knowing how: *know-how.* The question *what* is relatively insignificant. As long as one knows *how*, the *what* will take care of itself. You just initiate the process, and keep it going

The *what* follows. In fact, the *how* tends more and more to determine the *what*.

The question *who* also turns out to be irrelevant except insofar as it is reducible to a *how*. That is to say that what matters is not the person so much as the position he occupies, the influence he wields, the money he makes, and his general usefulness in getting things done, or at least his place in the machinery of society. Thus a man is identified not by his character but by his function or by his income, not by what he is but by what he has. If he has nothing, he does not count, and what is done to him or with him ceases to be a matter of ethical concern.

Pragmatism and positivism are therefore interested in the question *how*. Traditional metaphysics, whether scholastic (realist) or idealist, is interested in the question *what* (the essence). Existentialism wants to know *who*. It is interested in the authentic use of freedom by the concrete personal subject.

The Visionary Art of Flannery O'Connor

by Joyce Carol Oates

...something is developing in the world by means of us,
perhaps at our expense.

— TEILHARD DE CHARDIN

The greatest of Flannery O'Connor's books is her last, post-humously-published collection of stories, *Everything That Rises Must Converge*. Though it is customary to interpret O'Connor's allusion to the philosophy of Teilhard de Chardin as ironic, it seems to me that there is no irony involved. There are many small ironies in these nine stories, certainly, and they are comic-grotesque and flamboyant and heartbreaking—but no ultimate irony is intended and the book is not a tragic one. It is a collection of revelations; like all revelations, it points to a dimension of experiential truth that lies outside the sphere of the questing, speculative mind, but which is nevertheless available to all.

The "psychic interpenetrability" of which Teilhard speaks in *The Phenomenon of Man* determines that man, in "rising" to a higher consciousness, will of necessity coalesce into a unity that is basically a phenomenon of mind (hence of man, since only man possesses self-consciousness). It is misleading to emphasize Teilhard's optimism at the expense of his cautious consideration of what he calls the "doctrine by isolation"[1] and the "cynical and brutal theories" of the contemporary world; O'Connor has

"The Visionary Art of Flannery O'Connor" by Joyce Carol Oates. From *Southern Humanities Review*, vol. 7, no. 3 (Summer, 1973), pp. 235-246. Reprinted by permission of *Southern Humanities Review*.

[1]Pierre Teilhard de Chardin, *The Phenomenon of Man* (New York, 1959), p. 262.

dramatized the tragic consequences of the locked-in ego in earlier fiction, but in *Everything That Rises Must Converge* nearly every story addresses itself to the problem of bringing to consciousness the latent horror, making manifest the Dream of Reason—which is of course a nightmare. It is a measure of her genius that she can so easily and so skillfully evoke the spiritual while dealing in a very concrete, very secular world of fragmentary people.

Despite her rituals of baptism-by-violence, and her apparently merciless subjecting of ordinary "good" people to extraordinary fates, O'Connor sees the world as an incarnation of spirit; she has stated that the art of fiction itself is "very much an incarnational art."[2] In a way she shares the burdens of her fanatical preachers Motes and Tarwater: she sees herself as writing from a prophetic vision, as a "realist of distances."[3] Her people are not quite whole until violence makes them whole. They must suffer amazing initiations, revelations nearly as physically brutal as those in Kafka—one might explore the similarities between Parker of "Parker's Back" and the heroic, doomed officer of "In The Penal Colony"—because their way into the spiritual is through the physical; the way into O'Connor's dimension of the sacred is through the secular or vulgar. Teilhard's rising of consciousness into a mysterious Super-Life, in which the multiplicity of the world's fragments are driven to seek one another through love assumes a mystical "gravity of bodies"[4] that must have appealed to O'Connor's sacramental imagination. Fundamental to the schoolteacher Rayber's insistence upon rationality is his quite justified terror of the Unconscious—he must act out of his thinking, calculating, mechanical ego simply in order to resist the gravity that threatens to carry him out of himself; otherwise, he will become another "fanatic," another victim of that love that is hidden in the blood, in this specific instance in terms of Christ. The local, human tragedy is, then, the highly conscious resisting of the Incarnation. As human beings (who are fragments) resist the gravity that should bring them into a unity, they emphasize their isolation, their helplessness, and can be delivered from the trance of Self only by violence.

[2]Flannery O'Connor, *Mystery and Manners* (New York, 1969), p. 68.
[3]*Ibid.*, p. 44.
[4]Teilhard, p. 291.

Paradoxically, the way into O'Connor's vision that is least ambiguous is through a story that has not received much attention, "The Lame Shall Enter First." This fifty-seven-page story is a reworking of the nuclear fable of *The Violent Bear It Away* and, since O'Connor explored the tensions between the personalities of the Rationalist-Liberal and the object of his charity at such length in the novel, she is free to move swiftly and bluntly here. "We are accustomed to consider," says Teilhard in a discussion of the energies of love "Beyond the Collective," "only the sentimental face of love. ...."[5] In "The Lame Shall Enter First" it is this sentimental love that brings disaster to the would-be Savior, Sheppard. He is a young, white-haired City Recreational Director who, on Saturdays, works as a counselor at a boys reformatory; since his wife's death he has moved out of their bedroom and lives an ascetic, repressed life, refusing even to fully acknowledge his love for his son. Befriending the crippled, exasperating Rufus Johnson, Sheppard further neglects his own son, Norton, and is forced to realize that his entire conception of himself has been hypocritical. O'Connor underscores the religious nature of his experience by calling it a *revelation:* Sheppard hears his own voice "as if it were the voice of his accuser." Though he closes his eyes against the revelation, he cannot elude it:

> His heart contracted with a repulsion for himself so clear and so intense that he gasped for breath. He had stuffed his own emptiness with good works like a glutton. He had ignored his own child to feed his vision of himself. He saw the clear-eyed Devil, the sounder of hearts, leering at him. ... His image of himself shrivelled until everything was black before him. He sat there paralyzed, aghast.

Sheppard then wakes from his trance and runs to his son, but, even as he hurries to the boy, he imagines Norton's face "transformed; the image of his salvation; all light," and the reader sees that even at this dramatic point Sheppard is deluded. It is still *his* salvation he desires, *his* experience of the transformation of his son's misery into joy. Therefore it is poetically just that his

[5]*Ibid.,* p. 290.

change of heart leads to nothing, to no joyous reconciliation. He rushes up to the boy's room and discovers that Norton has hanged himself.

The boy's soul has been "launched...into space"; like Bishop of *The Violent Bear It Away* he is a victim of the tensions between two ways of life, two warring visions. In the image of Christ there is something "mad" and "stinking" and catastrophic, at least in a secularized civilization; in the liberal, manipulative humanitarianism of the modern world there is that "clear-eyed Devil" that cuts through all bonds, all mystery, all "psychical convergence" that cannot be reduced to simplistic sociological formulas. It is innocence that is destroyed. The well-intentioned Savior, Sheppard, has acted only to fill his own vacuity; his failure as a true father results in his son's suicide.

> He had stuffed his own emptiness with good works like a glutton.

Perhaps this is O'Connor's judgment, blunt and final, upon our civilization. Surely she is sympathetic with Teilhard's rejection of egoism, as the last desperate attempt of the world of matter— in its fragmentary forms, "individuals"—to persist in its own limited being. In discussing the evolutionary process of love, the rising-to-consciousness of individuals through love, Teilhard analyzes the motives for "the fervour and impotence" that accompany every egoistic solution of life:

> In trying to separate itself as much as possible from others, the element individualises itself; but in so doing it becomes retrograde and seeks to drag the world backwards toward plurality and into matter. In fact it diminishes itself and loses itself. ... The peak of ourselves, the acme of our originality, is not our individuality but our person; and according to the evolutionary structure of the world, we can only find our person by uniting together.[6]

What is difficult, perhaps, is to see how the humanitarian impulse —when it is not spiritual—is an egoistic activity. O'Connor's imagination is like Dostoyevsky's: politically reactionary, but spiritually fierce, combative, revolutionary. If the liberal, atheistic, man-centered society of modern times is dedicated to manipulating others in order to "save" them, to transform them into

---

[6]*Ibid.*, p. 289.

flattering images of their own egoes, then there is no love in-volved—there is no true merging of selves, but only a manipula-tive aggression. This kind of love is deadly, because it believes itself to be selfless; it is the sudden joy of the intellectual Julian, in the story "Everything That Rises Must Converge," when he sees that his mother is about to be humiliated by a black woman who is wearing the same outrageously ugly hat his mother has bought—"His grin hardened until it said to her as plainly as if he were saying aloud: Your punishment exactly fits your pettiness. This should teach you a permanent lesson." The lesson his mother gets, however, is fatal: the permanence of death.

"He thinks he's Jesus Christ!" the club-footed juvenile de-linquent, Rufus Johnson, exclaims of Sheppard. He thinks he is divine, when in fact he is empty; he tries to stuff himself with what he believes to be good works, in order to disguise the terrifying fact of his own emptiness. For O'Connor *this* is the gravest sin. Her madmen, thieves, misfits, and murderers commit crimes of a secular nature, against other men; they are not so sinful as the criminals who attempt to usurp the role of the divine. In Kafka's words, "They...attempted to realize the happiness of mankind without the aid of grace."[7] It is an erecting of the Tower of Babel upon the finite, earthly Wall of China: a ludicrous act of folly.

O'Connor's writing is stark and, for many readers, difficult to absorb into a recognizable world, because it insists upon a brutal distinction between what Augustine would call the City of Man and the City of God. One can reject O'Connor's fierce insistence upon this separation—as I must admit I do—and yet sympathize with the terror that must be experienced when these two "realms" of being are imagined as distinct. For, given the essentially Manichean dualism of the Secular and the Sacred, man is forced to choose between them: he cannot comfortably live in both "cities." Yet his body, especially if it is a diseased and obviously, immediately, *perpetually* mortal body, forces him to realize that he is existing in that City of Man, at every instant that he is not so spiritually chaste as to be in the City of God. Therefore life is a struggle; the natural, ordinary world is either sacramental (and ceremonial) or profane (and vulgar). And it follows from this that the diseased body is not only an affirmation, or a symbolic inten-

[7]Gustav Janouch, *Conversations With Kafka* (New York, 1971), p. 90.

sification of, the spiritual "disease" that attends physical processes; it becomes a matter of one's personal salvation—Jung
would use the term "individuation'—to interpret the accidents of
the flesh in terms of the larger, unfathomable, but ultimately *no
more abstract* pattern that links the Self to the Cosmos. This is a
way of saying that for Flannery O'Connor (as for Kafka and for
D. H. Lawrence) the betrayal of the body, its loss of normal
health, must be seen as necessary; it must make sense. *Wise
Blood,* ironically begun before O'Connor suffered her first at-
tack of the disease that ultimately killed her, a disease inherited
from her father, makes the point dramatically and lyrically that
the "blood" is "wise". And rebellion is futile against it. Thus, the
undulant fever suffered by the would-be writer, Asbury, is not
only directly and medically attributable to *his* rash behavior
(drinking unpasteurized milk, against his mother's rules of the
dairy), but it becomes the means by which he realizes a revelation
he would not otherwise have experienced. Here, O'Connor affirms a far more primitive and far more brutal sense of fate than
Teilhard would affirm—at least as I understand Teilhard—for in
the physical transformation of man into a higher consciousness
and finally into a collective, god-like "synthesized state"[8] the
transformation is experienced in terms of a space/time series of
events, but is in fact (if it could be a demonstrable or measurable
"fact") one single event: one phenomenon. Therefore, the "physical" is not really a lower form of the spiritual, but is experienced
as being lower, or earlier in evolution, and the fear of or con-
tempt for the body expressed by Augustine is simply a confusion.
The physical is also spiritual; the physical only seems not to be
"spiritual." Though this sounds perplexing, it is really a way of
saying that Augustine (and perhaps O'Connor, who was very
much influenced by Augustine and other Catholic theologians)
prematurely denied the sacredness of the body, as if it were a
hindrance and not the only means by which the spirit can attain
its "salvation." Useless to rage against his body's deterioration,
Lawrence says sadly, and nobly, because that body was the only
means by which D. H. Lawrence could have appeared in the
world. But this is not at all what O'Connor does, for in her necessary and rather defiant acceptance of her inherited disease in

[8]Teilhard, p. 309.

terms of its being, perhaps, a kind of Original Sin and therefore
not an accident—somehow obscurely willed either by God or by
O'Connor herself (if we read "The Enduring Chill" as a metaphor
for O'Connor's predicament)—we are forced to affirm the disease-
as-revelation:

> The boy [Asbury] fell back on his pillow and stared at the ceiling.
> His limbs that had been racked for so many weeks by fever and
> chill were numb now. The old life in him was exhausted. He
> awaited the coming of new. It was then that he felt the beginning of
> a chill, a chill so peculiar, so light, that it was like a warm ripple
> across a deeper sea of cold. ... Asbury blanched and the last film of
> illusion was torn as if by a whirlwind from his eyes. He saw that for
> the rest of his days, frail, racked, but enduring, he would live in the
> face of a purifying terror. A feeble cry, a last impossible protest
> escaped him. But the Holy Ghost, emblazoned in ice instead of fire,
> continued, implacable, to descend.   ("The Enduring Chill")

This particular story and its epiphany may not have the aesthetic power to move us that belong to O'Connor's more sharply-
imagined works, but it is central to an understanding of all of her
writing and, like Lawrence's "The Ship of Death," it has a beauty
and a terrible dignity that carry it beyond criticism. For while
Teilhard's monumental work stresses the uniqueness of the individual through his absorption in a larger, and ultimately
divine, "ultimate earth," there cannot be in his work the dramatization of the real, living, bleeding, suffering, *existing* individual
that O'Connor knows so well. She knows this existing individual
from the inside and not from the outside; she knows that while
the historical and sociological evolution causes one group of
people to "rise" (the blacks; the haughty black woman in "Everything That Rises Must Converge"), it is also going to destroy
others (both Julian and his mother, who evidently suffers a stroke
when the black woman hits her), and she also knows—it is this
point, I believe, missed by those critics who are forever stressing
her 'irony'—that *the entire process is divine.* Hence her superficially reactionary attitude toward the secularized, liberal, Godless society, and her affirmation of the spontaneous, the irrational,
the wisdom of the blood in which, for her, Christ somehow is
revealed. Because she does believe and states clearly[9] that her

[9]In the essay "The Fiction Writer and His Country," she declares "for me the
meaning of life is centered in our Redemption by Christ." *Mystery and Manners,* p. 32.

writing is an expression of her religious commitment, and is itself a kind of divine distortion ("the kind that reveals, or should
reveal," as she remarks in the essay "Novelist and Believer"), the
immediate problem for most critics is *how* to wrench her work
away from her, *how* to show that she didn't at all know herself,
but must be subjected to a higher, wiser, more objective consciousness in order to be understood. But the amazing thing
about O'Connor is that she seems to have known exactly what she
was doing and how she might best accomplish it. There is no ultimate irony in her work, no ultimate despair or pessimism or
tragedy, and certainly not a paradoxical sympathy for the Devil.[10]
It is only when O'Connor is judged from a secular point of view,
or from a "rational" point of view, that she seems unreasonable—
a little mad—and must be chastely revised by the liberal imagination.

"Everything That Rises Must Converge" is a story in which
someone appears to lose, and to lose mightily; but the "loss" is
fragmentary, a necessary and minor part of the entire process of
"converging" that is the entire universe—or God. The son, Julian,
is then released to the same "entry into the world of guilt and sorrow" that is Rayber's, and Sheppard's, and his surrender to the
emotions he has carefully refined into ironic, cynical, "rational"
ideas is at the same time his death (as an enlightened Ego) and
his birth (as a true adult). Many of the stories in this volume deal
literally with the strained relationships between one generation
and another, because this is a way of making explicit the psychological problem of ascending to a higher self. In *A Good Man is
Hard to Find* the tensions were mainly between strangers and in
term of very strange gods. The life you save may be your own,
and if you cannot bear the realization that a freak is a Temple of
the Holy Ghost, that is unfortunate for you. As Rufus Johnson
says of the Bible, superbly and crazily, *Even if I didn't believe it,
it would still be true*—a reply to infuriate the rationalist Sheppard,
and no doubt most of us! But O'Connor's art is both an existential
dramatization of what it means to suffer, and to suffer intelligent-
ly, coherently, and a deliberate series of parodies of that subjec-
tivist philosophy loosely called "existentialism"—though it is the
solipsistic, human-value-oriented existentialism she obviously

---

[10]See John Hawkes' essay, "Flannery O'Connor's Devil," *Sewanee Review*,
LXX (Summer, 1962), p. 400.

despises, Sartrean and not Kierkegaardian. The Deist may say "Whatever is, is right," but the Deist cannot prove the truth of his statement, for such truths or revelations can only be experienced by an existing, suffering individual whom some violent shock has catapulted into the world of sorrow. When the intellectual Julian suffers the real loss of his mother, the real Julian emerges; his self-pitying depression vanishes at once; the faith he had somehow lost "in the midst of his martyrdom" is restored. So complex and so powerful a story cannot be reduced to any single meaning; but it is surely O'Connor's intention to show how the egoistic Julian is a spokesman for an entire civilization, and to demonstrate the way by which this civilization will—inevitably, horribly—be jolted out of its complacent, wordly cynicism. *By violence.* And by no other way, because the Ego cannot be destroyed except violently, it cannot be argued out of its egoism by words, by any logical argument, it cannot be instructed in anything except a physical manner. O'Connor would have felt a kinship with the officer of Kafka's "In the Penal Colony," who yearns for an enlightenment that can only come through his own body, through a sentence tattooed on his body. As Christ suffered with his real, literal body, so O'Connor's people must suffer in order to realize Christ in them.

Yet it is not finally necessary to share O'Connor's specific religious beliefs in order to appreciate her art. Though she would certainly refute me in saying this, the "Christ" experience itself may well be interpreted as a psychological event which is received by the individual according to his private expectations. No writer obsessively works and re-works a single theme that is without deep personal meaning, so it is quite likely that O'Connor experienced mystical "visions" or insights, which she interpreted according to her Catholicism; her imagination was visual and literal, and she is reported to have said of the Eucharist that if it were only a symbol, "I'd say the hell with it."[11] This child-like or primitive rejection of a psychic event—*only* a symbol!—as if it were somehow less real than a physical event gives to O'Connor's writing that curious sense of blunt, graphic impatience, the either/or of fanaticism and genius, that makes it difficult for even

[11]Quoted by Robert Fitzgerald in his introduction to *Everything That Rises Must Converge* (New York, 1965), p. xiii.

her most sympathetic critics to relate her to the dimension of psychological realism explored by the traditional novel. Small obscenities or cruelties in the work of John Updike, for instance, have a power to upset us in a way that gross fantastic acts of violence in O'Connor do not, for we read O'Connor as a writer of parables and Updike as an interpreter of the way we actually live. Yet, because she is impatient with the City of Man except as it contrasts with the City of God, she can relate her localized horrors to a larger harmony that makes everything, however exaggerated, somehow contained within a compact vision.

The triumph of "Revelation" is its apparently natural unfolding of a series of quite extraordinary events, so that the impossibly smug, self-righteous Mrs. Turpin not only experiences a visual revelation but is prepared for it, demands it, and is equal to it in spite of her own bigotry. Another extraordinary aspect of the story is the protagonist's assumption—an almost automatic assumption— that the vicious words spoken to her by a deranged girl in a doctor's waiting room ("Go back to hell where you came from, you old wart hog") are in fact the words of Christ, intended for her alone. Not only is the spiritual world a literal, palpable fact, but the physical world—of other people, of objects and events—becomes transparent, only a means by which the "higher" judgment is delivered. It is a world of meanings, naturalistic details crowded upon one another until they converge into a higher significance; an anti-naturalistic technique, perhaps, but one which is firmly based in the observed world. O'Connor is always writing about Original Sin and the ways we may be delivered from it, and therefore she does not—cannot—believe in the random innocence of naturalism, which states that all men are innocent and are victims of inner or outer accidents. The naturalistic novel, which attempts to render the "real" world in terms of its external events, must hypothesize an interior randomness that is a primal innocence, antithetical to the Judaeo-Christian culture. O'Connor uses many of the sharply-observed surfaces of the world, but her medieval sense of the *correspondentia* or the ancient "sympathy of all things" forces her to severely restrict her subject matter, compressing it to one or two physical settings and a few hours' duration. Since revelation can occur at any time and sums up, at the same time that it eradicates, all of

a person's previous life, there is nothing claustrophobic about the
doctor's waiting room, "which was very small," but which becomes a microcosm of an entire Godless society.

"Revelation" falls into two sections. The first takes place in
the doctor's waiting room; the second takes place in a pig barn.
Since so many who live now are diseased, it is significant that
O'Connor chooses a doctor's waiting room for the first half of Mrs.
Turpin's revelation, and it is significant that gospel hymns are
being played over the radio, almost out of earshot, incorporated
into the mechanical vacant listlessness of the situation: "When I
looked up and He looked down... And wona these days I know
I'll we-eara crown." Mrs. Turpin glances over the room, notices
white-trashy people who are "worse than niggers any day," and
begins a conversation with a well-dressed lady who is accompany-
ing her daughter: the girl, on the verge of a breakdown, is reading a book called *Human Development,* and it is this book which
will strike Mrs. Turpin in the forehead. Good Christian as she
imagines herself, Mrs. Turpin cannot conceive of human beings
except in terms of class, and is obsessed by a need to continually
categorize others and speculate upon her position in regard to
them. The effort is so exhausting that she often ends up dreaming "they were all crammed in together in a box car, being ridden
off to be put in a gas oven." O'Connor's chilling indictment of
Mrs. Turpin's kind of Christianity grows out of her conviction
that the displacement of Christ will of necessity result in murder,
but that the "murder" is a slow steady drifting rather than a conscious act of will.

The ugly girl, blue-faced with acne, explodes with rage at the
inane bigotry expressed by Mrs. Turpin, and throws the textbook at her. She loses all control and attacks her; held down, subdued, her face "churning," she seems to Mrs. Turpin to know her
"in some intense and personal way, beyond time and place and
condition." And the girl's eyes lighten, as if a door that had been
tightly closed was now open "to admit light and air." Mrs. Turpin
steels herself, as if awaiting a revelation: and indeed the revelation
comes. Mary Grace, used here by O'Connor as the instrument
through which Christ speaks, bears some resemblance to other
misfits in O'Connor's stories—not the rather stylish, shabby-
glamorish men, but the pathetic over-educated physically un-
attractive girls like Joy/Hulga of "Good Country People." That

O'Connor identifies with these girls is obvious; it is *she*, through Mary Grace, who throws that textbook on human development at all of us, striking us in the forehead, hopefully to bring about a change in our lives.

Mrs. Turpin is shocked, but strangely courageous. It is rare in O'Connor that an obtuse, unsympathetic character ascends to a higher level of self-awareness; indeed she shows more courage than O'Connor's intellectual young men. She has been called a wart hog from hell and her vision comes to her in the pig barn, where she stands above the hogs that appear to "pant with a secret life." It is these hogs, the secret panting mystery of life itself, that finally allow Mrs. Turpin to realize her vision. She seems to absorb from them some "abysmal life-giving knowledge" and, at sunset, she stares into the sky where she sees

> a vast swinging bridge extending upward from the earth through a field of living fire. Upon it a vast horde of souls were rumbling toward heaven. There were whole companies of white-trash, clean for the first time in their lives, and bands of black niggers in white robes, and battalions of freaks and lunatics shouting and clapping and leaping like frogs. And bringing up the end of the procession was a tribe of people whom she recognized at once as those who, like herself and Claude, had always had a little of everything. . . . They were marching behind the others with great dignity, accountable as they always had been for good order and common sense and respectable behavior. They alone were on key. Yet she could see by their shocked and altered faces that even their virtues were being burned away. . . .

This is the most powerful of O'Connor's revelations, because it questions the very foundations of our assumptions of the ethical life. It is not simply our "virtues" that will be burned away, but our rational faculties as well, and perhaps even the illusion of our separate, isolated egos. There is no way in which the ego can confront Mrs. Turpin's vision, except as she does—"her eyes small but fixed unblinkingly on what lay ahead." Like Teilhard, O'Connor is ready to acquiesce to the evolution of a form of higher consciousness that may be forcing itself into the world *at our expense;* as old Tarwater says, after he is struck and silenced by fire, "even the mercy of the Lord burns." Man cannot remain what he is; he cannot exist without being transformed. We are

confronted, says Teilhard, with two directions and only two: one
upward and the other downward.

> Either nature is closed to our demands for futurity, in which case
> thought, the fruit of millions of years of effort, is stifled, still-
> born in a self-abortive and absurd universe. Or else an opening
> exists—that of the super-soul above our souls; but in that case the
> way out, if we are to agree to embark upon it, must open out freely
> onto limitless psychic spaces in a universe to which we can un-
> hesitatingly entrust ourselves.[12]

O'Connor's people are forced into the upward direction, sometimes against their wills, sometimes because their wills have been
burned clean and empty. Rayber *(The Violent Bear It Away)*,
who has concentrated his love for mankind into a possessive,
exaggerated love for an idiot child, is forced to contemplate a
future without the "raging pain, the intolerable hurt that was his
due"; he is at the core of O'Connor's vision, a human being who
has suffered a transformation but who survives. The wisdom of
the body speaks in us, even when it reveals to us a terrifying
knowledge of Original Sin, a perversion of the blood itself.

O'Connor's revelations concern the mystic origin of religious
experience, absolutely immune to any familiar labels of "good"
and "evil." Her perverted saints are Kierkegaardian knights of
the "absurd" for whom ordinary human behavior is impossible.
Like young Tarwater, horrified at having said an obscenity, they
are "too fierce to brook impurities of such a nature"; they are,
like O'Connor herself, "intolerant of unspiritual evils. ..." There
is no patience in O'Connor for a systematic, refined, rational acceptance of God; and of the gradual transformation of apocalyptic
religious experience into dogma, she is strangely silent. Her
world is that surreal primitive landscape in which the Unconscious is a determining quantity that the Conscious cannot defeat.
because it cannot recognize. In fact, there is nothing to be recognized—there is only, an experience to be suffered.[13]

[12]Teilhard, p. 256.
[13]Flannery O'Connor is a remarkable synthesis of what Jung would call the
personality characterized by *participation mystique* and that personality that
"suffers in the lower stories, so to speak, but in the upper stories is singularly
detached from painful as well as joyful events." ("Commentary on *The Secret of
the Golden Flower,*" in Jung's *Psyche and Symbol* (New York, 1958), p. 340.)

Chronology of Important Dates

1849   Sarah Orne Jewett born in South Berwick, Maine, on September 3.

1862   Edith Wharton (Edith Newbold Jones) born in New York on January 24.

1873   Willa Sibert Cather born in Virginia near Winchester on December 7.

1877   *Deephaven* (Jewett).

1882   Jewett takes her first of many trips abroad with her lifelong companion, Annie Adams Fields, the widow of a prominent Boston publisher.

1883   Cather family emigrates to a ranch in Nebraska.

1884   *A Country Doctor* (Jewett).

1885   *A Marsh Island* (Jewett).
Edith Newbold Jones marries Edward Robbins Wharton of Boston.

1886   *A White Heron and Other Stories* (Jewett).

1888   *The King of Folly Island and Other People* (Jewett).

1890   Katherine Anne Porter born in Indian Creek, Texas, on May 15. After the death of her mother in 1892, the family moves to live with her paternal grandmother, Catherine Anne Porter, who dies in 1901.

1893   *A Native of Winby and Other Tales* (Jewett).

1895   *The Life of Nancy* (Jewett).

1896   *The Country of the Pointed Firs* (Jewett).

*Indicates short story collection.

1899   *The Greater Inclination* (Wharton).

1901   *The Tory Lover* (Jewett); *Crucial Instances* (Wharton).
            Jewett awarded the first honorary Litt.D. granted by Bowdoin
            College to a woman.

1902   *The Valley of Decision* (Wharton).

1903   *April Twilights* (Cather, poems).

1904   *The Descent of Man* (Wharton).

1905   *The House of Mirth* (Wharton); *The Troll Garden* (Cather).

1906   Cather begins her six years of work for *McClure's Magazine*
            in New York.
            Porter runs away from school, marries, and is divorced after
            three years.

1907   *The Fruit of the Tree* (Wharton).

1908   *The Hermit and the Wild Woman* (Wharton).
            Cather meets Jewett at the home of Mrs. Fields in Boston.

1909   Eudora Alice Welty born in Jackson, Mississippi on April 13.
            Sarah Orne Jewett dies of a stroke in Maine on June 24.

1910   *Tales of Men and Ghosts* (Wharton).
            The Whartons sell their house in Lenox, Massachusetts, and
            move to France, where Edward Wharton has a nervous break-
            down and is placed in a sanatorium.

1911   *Ethan Frome* (Wharton).

1912   *The Reef* (Wharton); *Alexander's Bridge* (Cather).
            Cather visits ruins of ancient cliff dwellers in Arizona for the
            first time.

1913   *The Custom of the Country* (Wharton); *O Pioneers!* (Cather).
            Edith Wharton granted a divorce.

1915   *The Song of the Lark* (Cather).

1916   *Verses* (Jewett, posthumously collected); *Xingu and Other
            Stories* (Wharton).

1917   *Summer* (Wharton).

1918   *My Ántonia* (Cather).

            *Indicates short story collection.

1920   *The Age of Innocence* (Wharton), awarded Pulitzer Prize;
        *Youth and the Bright Medusa (Cather).
        Porter studies art in Mexico, a country that will remain impor-
        tant in her life for at least the next ten years.

1922   *One of Ours* (Cather), awarded Pulitzer Prize.

1923   *A Lost Lady* (Cather).

1925   Flannery O'Connor born in Savannah, Georgia on March 25.
        The Writing of Fiction (Wharton); *The Professor's House*
        (Cather).

1926   *My Mortal Enemy* (Cather).

1927   *Twilight Sleep* (Wharton); *Death Comes for the Archbishop*
        (Cather).

1928   *The Children* (Wharton).

1930   **Flowering Judas* (Porter).

1931   *Shadows on the Rock* (Cather).

1932   **Obscure Destinies* (Cather).

1933   Porter marries Eugene Pressly, a member of the American
        Foreign Service. She is divorced in 1938.

1934   *A Backward Glance* (Wharton); "Hacienda" (Porter).

1935   *Lucy Gayheart* (Cather).

1937   Edith Wharton dies of apoplectic stroke in France on August
        11. Her many awards include being the first woman to re-
        ceive an honorary Litt.D. from Yale and the first to receive
        two Pulitzers [for *The Age of Innocence* and *The Old Maid*, a
        play version of a 1924 short novel] .

1938   *The Buccaneers* (Wharton, unfinished).
        Porter marries Albert Russel Erskine, Jr., a member of the
        Louisiana State University faculty. She is divorced in 1942.

1939   **Pale Horse, Pale Rider* (Porter).

1940   *Sapphira and the Slave Girl* (Cather).

1941   **A Curtain of Green and Other Stories* (Welty).

        *Indicates short story collection.

1942   *The Robber Bridegroom* (Welty).

1943   **The Wide Net and Other Stories* (Welty).

1944   **The Leaning Tower, and Other Stories* (Porter).

1946   *Delta Wedding* (Welty).

1947   Willa Cather dies of cerebral hemorrhage in New York on April 24.

1948   **The Old Beauty and Others* (Cather, posthumously published); **Music From Spain* (Welty).

1949   **The Golden Apples* (Welty).

1952   *The Days Before* (Porter, essays); *Wise Blood* (O'Connor).

1954   *The Ponder Heart* (Welty), awarded the Howells Medal in 1955.

1955   **The Bride of the Innisfallen and Other Stories* (Welty); *A Good Man Is Hard to Find* (O'Connor).

1960   *The Violent Bear It Away* (O'Connor).

1962   *Ship of Fools* (Porter).

1964   *The Shoe Bird* (Welty).
          Flannery O'Connor dies of lupus in Milledgeville, Georgia, on August 3.

1965   **Everything That Rises Must Converge* (O'Connor, posthumously published); **The Collected Stories of Katherine Anne Porter.*

1966   Porter receives both the Pulitzer Prize and the National Book Award for Fiction for her *Collected Stories.*

1969   *Mystery and Manners* (O'Connor, essays).

1970   *The Collected Essays and Occasional Writings of Katherine Anne Porter; Losing Battles* (Welty).

1972   *The Optimist's Daughter* (Welty), awarded Pulitzer Prize.

1978   *The Eye of the Story* (Welty, selected essays and reviews).

1979   *The Habit of Being* (O'Connor, letters edited by Sally Fitzgerald).

          *Indicates short story collection.

Notes on the Editor and Contributors

HEATHER McCLAVE, born in 1946, teaches English and American literature at Harvard University and is writing a book on Dickinson, Frost, Stevens, and Eliot.

WARNER BERTHOFF, born in 1925, is Professor of English and American literature at Harvard University and author of *The Example of Melville, The Ferment of Realism: American Literature, 1884-1919*, and *Edmund Wilson.*

RICHARD WARRINGTON BALDWIN LEWIS, born in 1917, is Professor of English and American studies at Yale University and author of several books, including *The American Adam, The Picaresque Saint,* and *Edith Wharton: A Biography.*

KATHERINE ANNE PORTER: See Chronology in this volume.

LIONEL TRILLING (1905-1975) was one of the most distinguished and admired twentieth-century critics. A Professor of English at Columbia University for many years, he wrote numerous books, including *Matthew Arnold, The Liberal Imagination, The Opposing Self, Freud and the Crisis of Our Culture,* and *Beyond Culture.*

ROBERT PENN WARREN, born in 1905, Professor of English Emeritus at Yale, is an eminent man of letters—novelist, poet, critic, short story writer, dramatist—who to date has published ten novels, twelve volumes of poetry, and various critical studies.

EUDORA WELTY: See Chronology in this volume.

ALUN R. JONES teaches at the University of Wales in Bangor and is the author of *The Life and Opinions of T.E. Hulme.*

ROBERT FITZGERALD, born in 1910, is Boylston Professor of Rhetoric and Oratory at Harvard University. He is a distinguished poet and translator of the *Iliad,* the *Odyssey,* and various works by Sophocles, Euripides, and St.-John Perse.

Sister Mary Bernetta Quinn, O.S.F., born in 1915, is Professor of English at the College of Saint Teresa and author of *The Metamorphic Tradition in Modern Poetry* and *Ezra Pound: An Introduction to the Poetry.*

Thomas Merton (1915-1968) was a prolific and influential religious thinker best known for his poetry, his many collections of essays, including *Thoughts in Solitude* and *Zen and the Birds of Appetite,* and his autobiography, *The Seven Storey Mountain.*

Joyce Carol Oates, born in 1938, teaches English at the University of Windsor, Ontario, and writes fiction, poetry, and criticism on a wide variety of subjects.

Selected Bibliography

SARAH ORNE JEWETT

Cary, Richard, ed., *Appreciation of Sarah Orne Jewett.* Waterville, Maine: Colby College Press, 1973.

Green, David Bonnell, ed., *The World of Dunnet Landing.* Lincoln: University of Nebraska Press, 1962.

Matthiessen, F.O., *Sarah Orne Jewett.* Boston: Houghton Mifflin, 1929.

EDITH WHARTON

Auchincloss, Louis, *Edith Wharton.* Minneapolis: University of Minnesota Press, 1961.

Edel, Leon, "Edith Wharton" in *The Dictionary of American Biography,* Vol. 22. New York: Scribner's, 1958.

Kazin, Alfred, *On Native Ground.* New York: Reynal and Hitchcock, 1942.

Lewis, R.W.B., *Edith Wharton: A Biography.* New York: Harper & Row, Pub., 1975.

Lubbock, Percy, *Portrait of Edith Wharton.* Englewood Cliffs, N.J.: Prentice-Hall, 1947.

Nevius, Blake, *Edith Wharton, A Study of Her Fiction.* Berkeley and Los Angeles: University of California Press, 1953.

Wolff, Cynthia, *A Feast of Words: The Triumph of Edith Wharton.* New York: Oxford University Press, 1977.

WILLA CATHER

Brown, E.K., and Leon Edel, *Willa Cather: A Critical Biography,* New York: Knopf, 1953.

Lewis, Edith, *Willa Cather Living.* New York: Knopf, 1953.

Randall, John H., *The Landscape and the Looking Glass: Willa Cather's Search for Value.* Boston: Houghton Mifflin, 1960.

Schroeter, James, ed., *Willa Cather and Her Critics.* Ithaca, N.Y.: Cornell University Press, 1967.

KATHERINE ANNE PORTER

Hardy, John Edward, *Katherine Anne Porter.* New York: Ungar, 1973.

Hartley, Lodwick Charles, and George Core, eds., *Katherine Anne Porter: A Critical Symposium.* Athens: University of Georgia Press, 1969.

Warren, Robert Penn, ed., *Katherine Anne Porter: A Collection of Critical Essays.* Englewood Cliffs, N.J.: Prentice-Hall, 1979.

West, Ray B., Jr., "Katherine Anne Porter: Symbol and Theme in 'Flowering Judas,'" *Accent,* 7 (Spring 1947), 182-87.

Wilson, Edmund, "Katherine Anne Porter," *New Yorker,* 20 (September 30, 1944), 72-75.

EUDORA WELTY

Appel, Alfred, Jr., *A Season of Dreams: The Fiction of Eudora Welty.* Baton Rouge: Louisiana State University Press, 1965.

Porter, Katherine Anne, "Eudora Welty and 'A Curtain of Green,'" in *The Days Before.* New York: Harcourt Brace, 1952.

Shenandoah, 20 (Spring, 1969).

Vande Kieft, Ruth M., *Eudora Welty,* New York: Twayne, 1962.

FLANNERY O'CONNOR

Critique, no. 2 (Fall 1958).

Esprit, no. 1 (Winter 1964).

Friedman, M.J., and Lewis Lawson, eds., *The Added Dimension: The Art and Mind of Flannery O'Connor* (2nd ed.) New York: Fordham University Press, 1977.

Hawkes, John, "Flannery O'Connor's Devil," *Sewanee Review,* 70 (Summer 1962) 395-407.

Hendin, Josephine, *The World of Flannery O'Connor.* Bloomington: Indiana University Press, 1970.

Martin, Carter W., *The True Country: Themes in the Fiction of Flannery O'Connor.* Nashville, Tenn.: Vanderbilt University Press, 1969.

McClave, He

WOMEN WRITE

Spectrum Bo

171 pages